Mindful Motion: The Path to Lasting Mental Wellness

Gabriella Goldberger

Published by Azure Time Press, 2023.

While every precaution has been taken in the preparation of this book, the publisher assumes no responsibility for errors or omissions, or for damages resulting from the use of the information contained herein.

MINDFUL MOTION: THE PATH TO LASTING MENTAL WELLNESS

First edition. September 22, 2023.

ISBN: 979-8223479482

Written by Gabriella Goldberger.

Also by Gabriella Goldberger

Mindful Eating: Nourish Your Well-Being
Holistic Approaches to Stress Management
Nutrition and Immune Health
The Connection Between Sleep and Health
85 Remarkable Women in History
Mindful Motion: The Path to Lasting Mental Wellness

Table of Contents

To all those who have taken a step, both big and small, towards nurturing their mental wellness. Your journey is a testament to your resilience and your commitment to a brighter, healthier, and more fulfilled life. May this book be a guiding light on your path, and may your dedication inspire others to embark on their own transformative journeys.

Chapter 1: Introduction to the Mental Health-Physical Activity Connection

Understanding the Mind-Body Connection

In the bustling landscape of modern life, where stress and anxiety have become constant companions, it's easy to overlook the profound link between our physical bodies and our mental well-being. Yet, as we embark on this journey into the heart of the mental health-physical activity connection, we begin with a fundamental truth: the mind and body are deeply intertwined, each holding the key to the other's health and harmony.

Imagine your body as a finely tuned instrument, and your mind as the skilled musician. For the music to flow smoothly and harmoniously, both must be in sync. This is the essence of the mind-body connection.

The Symphony Within:

Picture yourself in a serene park on a crisp morning, taking your first steps on a nature trail. As you walk, your heart rate gently rises, and the oxygen-rich air fills your lungs. The sun's gentle rays warm your skin, and a sense of tranquility washes over you. You may have noticed something remarkable happening during this experience - your thoughts seem to clear, and your worries start to fade.

This is the mind-body connection in action, and it's more than just a pleasant feeling. When you engage in physical activity, your brain releases a cascade of chemicals known as neurotransmitters. Among these, serotonin, often called the "feel-good" neurotransmitter, surges in response to exercise. This boost in serotonin levels can lead to improved mood, reduced anxiety, and enhanced overall mental well-being.

Breaking Down Barriers:

Now, consider the opposite scenario - a sedentary lifestyle marked by prolonged periods of sitting, minimal physical activity, and a lack of engagement with the world around you. In such a state, the mind-body connection can become distorted, leading to a range of mental health challenges.

Studies have shown that individuals who lead predominantly sedentary lives are at a higher risk of developing conditions like depression and anxiety. This might seem counterintuitive at first, but the explanation is rooted in the biological effects of inactivity. When we sit for extended periods, our bodies don't produce the same beneficial chemicals as when we move. Over time, this imbalance can manifest as mood disturbances and cognitive decline.

A Two-Way Street:

The mind-body connection is not a one-way street. Just as physical activity influences mental health, our thoughts, emotions, and psychological state can, in turn, shape our physical well-being. Think about a time when stress or sadness felt like a heavy weight on your shoulders. These emotions can manifest physically, leading to muscle tension, sleep disturbances, and even chronic health conditions.

In this way, the mind and body converse continuously, impacting each other's health in a delicate dance. Recognizing this relationship is the first step towards harnessing its power for the betterment of our mental well-being.

The Path Forward:

As we delve deeper into the mental health-physical activity connection, we'll uncover the intricate ways in which exercise can positively impact not only our mood but also our ability to manage stress, overcome adversity, and build resilience. We'll hear inspiring stories of individuals who have harnessed the transformative potential of physical activity to heal and thrive.

So, dear reader, as you embark on this exploration with us, keep in mind that the mind-body connection is not a mere concept; it's a profound reality that holds the promise of better mental health. It's a journey worth taking, a symphony worth orchestrating, and a connection worth nurturing. Together, we'll uncover the power of physical activity to transform lives, one step at a time.

The Essence of Purpose:

At its core, "The Power of Physical Activity for Mental Health" seeks to illuminate a path toward enhanced mental well-being, forged through the medium of physical activity and exercise. It is a journey fueled by the desire to empower individuals like you with knowledge, inspiration, and actionable guidance. This book strives to be a beacon of hope for those who may be grappling with the shadows of mental health challenges, offering them a ray of light to follow.

A Ray of Light:

Mental health struggles are ubiquitous in today's world, affecting millions of lives. Be it the quiet battles waged in the solitude of one's thoughts or the more pronounced encounters with conditions like anxiety and depression, these challenges know no boundaries. They touch individuals across age, gender, and cultural lines, leaving an indelible mark on the fabric of society.

Yet, amidst these struggles, there exists an underutilized and immensely powerful resource—the transformative potential of physical activity. This book aims to unlock that potential, to reveal the profound healing and strengthening effects that regular exercise can have on the mind. It aspires to be a guiding star, helping individuals navigate their own personal journeys toward improved mental well-being.

A Blueprint for Transformation:

In the chapters that follow, you will find stories of resilience and change—narratives of individuals who have found solace, strength, and renewal through fitness. You will encounter scientific insights into the neurobiology of exercise and its impact on mood, stress reduction, and sleep. You will uncover practical strategies for overcoming the barriers that often hinder the initiation and maintenance of an exercise routine.

But this book is not just about knowledge; it's about action. It encourages you to find your own "why," to set meaningful goals, and to embark on a path of physical activity that resonates with your unique needs and aspirations. It offers guidance on selecting the right activities, establishing sustainable routines, and celebrating the small victories along the way.

A Call to Action:

As we delve deeper into the chapters ahead, remember that this book is not a passive observer of the mental health-physical activity connection. It is an invitation—a call to action. It challenges you to explore, to experiment, and to embrace the transformative power of movement. It beckons you to discover how physical activity can become a cornerstone of your mental well-being, a lifelong companion on your journey toward greater resilience and happiness.

So, as you continue your exploration, keep your purpose close to your heart. Let it guide you through these pages and beyond, into a world where the power of physical activity can illuminate even the darkest corners of the mind. With purpose as our compass, we embark on this journey together, bound by the shared conviction that better mental health is within reach, one step at a time.

The Catalyst of Change:

Physical activity, in all its forms, is a potent catalyst for change. It possesses the remarkable ability to influence our mental state, imparting a series of effects that can ripple through our lives. At its core, physical activity is more than just a series of movements—it's a therapeutic agent for the mind.

A Chemical Symphony:

The human brain is a complex and intricate orchestra of chemicals and neurotransmitters. When we engage in physical activity, this orchestra springs to life in remarkable ways. Endorphins, often referred to as "feel-good" hormones, flood our system, generating a sense of euphoria and happiness. This chemical symphony extends to the release of serotonin, which plays a pivotal role in regulating mood and reducing anxiety.

Moreover, physical activity can foster the growth of new brain cells and enhance neural connectivity, a phenomenon known as neuroplasticity. This neurogenesis and enhanced connectivity can lead to improved cognitive function, including better memory and sharper focus.

A Shield Against Stress:

In the turbulent seas of life, stress is an ever-present wave. However, physical activity can be our sturdy vessel, helping us navigate these waters with resilience. When we exercise, our bodies experience a stress response in the short term, but this serves as a valuable practice ground for the mind. Regular exposure to manageable stressors during exercise can actually train the brain to handle stress more effectively in daily life.

Moreover, physical activity can lead to the reduction of cortisol, the body's primary stress hormone. This reduction can translate into lower overall stress levels and a more balanced emotional state. Exercise, in essence, becomes a shield against the ravages of stress.

The Gateway to Restful Sleep:

Quality sleep is the cornerstone of mental health. Yet, many individuals grappling with mental health challenges often face sleep disturbances. Physical activity can act as a key to unlocking the gateway to restful sleep. Regular exercise helps regulate circadian rhythms, improving the timing and quality of sleep.

Additionally, the calming effects of exercise on the nervous system can soothe racing thoughts and anxiety, paving the way for a tranquil night's rest. For those wrestling with insomnia or other sleep disorders, physical activity can be a non-pharmacological remedy, offering the gift of peaceful slumber.

Empowerment and Self-Esteem:

Physical activity is more than a means to shape the body; it's a journey of self-discovery and empowerment. As individuals set and achieve fitness goals, they often experience an enhanced sense of self-esteem and self-worth. The process of pushing boundaries and breaking personal records can instill a profound belief in one's capabilities, both physically and mentally.

This boost in self-esteem can have a ripple effect, transcending the realm of fitness to positively impact other areas of life. As we strengthen our bodies, we also strengthen our minds, fostering a sense of resilience and self-assuredness.

A Beacon of Hope:

In our exploration of how physical activity can make a difference, it becomes abundantly clear that exercise is not a passive remedy but an active force for change. It is a beacon of hope in the sea of mental health challenges, offering solace to those who may be struggling.

Chapter 2: The Science Behind It All

The Neurobiology of Exercise and Mood

As we venture deeper into the exploration of the mental health-physical activity connection, we must don our scientist's hat and peer into the intricate workings of the brain. In this chapter, we delve into the fascinating realm of neurobiology to unravel how exercise, that seemingly simple act of movement, wields a profound influence over our mood and emotional well-being.

The Brain's Orchestra:

Our brains are complex orchestras of neurons, neurotransmitters, and intricate networks. They are the conductors of our emotional symphony, playing a pivotal role in shaping our moods, emotions, and overall mental well-being. To understand how exercise affects our mood, we must first understand the key players in this symphony.

Dopamine: The Reward Molecule:

One of the stars of the brain's orchestra is dopamine, often hailed as the "reward molecule." Dopamine is released in response to pleasurable experiences, and exercise is a potent trigger for its release. When you engage in physical activity, your brain showers you with a surge of dopamine, creating feelings of pleasure and reward.

This neurochemical response is responsible for the "runner's high" that many athletes and fitness enthusiasts describe—a state of euphoria and contentment that accompanies sustained, vigorous exercise. The release of dopamine can alleviate symptoms of depression and anxiety, providing a natural mood boost.

Serotonin: The Mood Regulator:

Serotonin, another vital player in our emotional symphony, is known as the "feel-good" neurotransmitter. It plays a crucial role in regulating mood and emotions. Exercise has been shown to increase the availability of serotonin in the brain, leading to an improved sense of well-being.

Individuals with conditions like depression often have imbalances in serotonin levels. Engaging in regular physical activity can help restore this balance, potentially alleviating depressive symptoms and reducing anxiety. The impact on serotonin is why exercise is often prescribed as a complementary therapy for those managing mood disorders.

Stress Reduction Through Exercise:

Stress is a constant companion in our lives, but exercise can serve as a powerful ally in managing its impact. When we face a stressful situation, our bodies enter a "fight or flight" response, releasing stress hormones like cortisol. However, regular exercise can help train the body to handle stress more effectively.

Exercise acts as a form of controlled stress—a stressor that the body can adapt to. When we engage in physical activity, our bodies learn to manage and recover from stress more efficiently. Over time, this training effect can lead to a reduction in baseline cortisol levels, resulting in lower overall stress levels.

The Neurogenesis Miracle:

In addition to its effects on neurotransmitters, exercise has a remarkable influence on the structure of the brain itself. A phenomenon known as neurogenesis occurs when new brain cells are generated. Physical activity, especially aerobic exercise, has been shown to promote neurogenesis, particularly in the hippocampus—a region crucial for learning and memory.

This means that exercise not only enhances mood and reduces stress but also supports cognitive function and mental resilience. It's a remarkable testament to the power of movement to shape not only our emotions but also our intellect.

A Symphony of Change:

In this chapter, we've glimpsed the neurobiological underpinnings of how exercise affects mood. Dopamine and serotonin, the brain's maestros of pleasure and mood regulation, are activated during physical activity. Stress hormones like cortisol are tamed through regular exercise. Neurogenesis creates new pathways for learning and memory.

As we journey forward in this exploration, keep in mind the orchestration of your brain's symphony. Understand that when you engage in physical activity, you are not just moving your body; you are composing a masterpiece of emotional and mental well-being. It's a symphony of change, and the baton is in your hands, ready to guide you towards a brighter and more harmonious mental state.

Dopamine: The Elixir of Pleasure and Reward:

Imagine the brain as a grand theater, and dopamine as the standing ovation from an appreciative audience. It's the chemical signal that tells us something remarkable has happened—a reward has been earned. Dopamine is the brain's way of saying, "Well done!"

When we engage in physical activity, dopamine is released in a joyful burst. This release is responsible for the feelings of pleasure and reward that accompany exercise. It's the rush of elation after conquering a challenging workout or the wave of contentment that washes over us during a long hike.

This surge of dopamine is why exercise enthusiasts often describe experiencing a "high" during and after physical activity—a state of euphoria that can counteract feelings of stress, anxiety, and depression. It's this reward system that makes exercise not just good for our bodies but also highly appealing to our brains.

Serotonin: The Mood Stabilizer and Regulator:

Serotonin, another prominent figure in the brain's cast of characters, is often dubbed the "feel-good" neurotransmitter. This role isn't merely hyperbole; serotonin genuinely plays a critical role in regulating mood and emotions.

When serotonin levels are balanced, we experience a sense of well-being, emotional stability, and a brighter outlook on life. However, imbalances in serotonin are often implicated in mood disorders like depression and anxiety. This is where exercise steps in as a formidable ally.

Engaging in physical activity triggers the release and uptake of serotonin in the brain. This flood of serotonin can lift our spirits and help maintain emotional equilibrium. It's like a natural mood stabilizer, creating a buffer against the lows of depression and the peaks of anxiety.

Exercise as a Mood Moderator:

Exercise, then, can be seen as a mood moderator, fine-tuning the delicate balance of neurotransmitters in our brains. It doesn't just provide momentary relief but sets the stage for sustained emotional well-being.

In the midst of life's challenges, exercise becomes a tool for maintaining equilibrium—a way to bolster serotonin levels when they dip and to boost dopamine when we need a lift. It's a dynamic interplay between the chemistry of our brains and the rhythm of our movements.

The Dance of Dopamine and Serotonin:

Picture a dance floor where dopamine and serotonin perform a graceful waltz. When we engage in physical activity, they take to the floor, twirling and gliding in harmony. The release of dopamine rewards our efforts, while the rise in serotonin soothes our emotions.

It's a dance that can transform a gray mood into one filled with vibrant colors. It can turn a stressful day into a serene evening. It's the chemistry of joy and well-being, choreographed by the music of exercise.

A Symphony of Wellness:

As we delve deeper into the chapters that follow, keep in mind the profound role played by dopamine and serotonin in shaping our emotional experiences. Understand that when you engage in physical activity, you're not just working up a sweat; you're conducting a symphony of wellness in your brain.

With each step, each rep, and each stretch, you are orchestrating a symphony of mood enhancement and emotional resilience. It's the magic of neurotransmitters, the alchemy of movement, and it's yours to harness as we continue our journey into the heart of the mental health-physical activity connection.

The Stress Response:

Imagine a primal scene where our ancestors roamed the savannah, faced with the looming threat of a predator. In such moments, our bodies would activate the "fight or flight" response, flooding the system with stress hormones like cortisol and adrenaline. This response was essential for survival.

Fast forward to the present day, and while the predators may have changed, our bodies' response to stress remains largely the same. Modern stressors, like work pressures, financial worries, and relationship conflicts, trigger the same physiological response as facing a wild animal.

Exercise as Controlled Stress:

Exercise, remarkably, mimics this "fight or flight" response in a controlled and beneficial manner. When you engage in physical activity, your heart rate increases, and your body experiences a stress response. This might seem counterintuitive—why would we willingly subject ourselves to stress?

The magic lies in the controlled nature of exercise. While exercise creates a temporary stress response, it also provides an opportunity for your body to practice dealing with stress in a safe environment. This training effect can lead to increased resilience when facing stressors in everyday life.

Lowering Cortisol Levels:

Cortisol, often dubbed the "stress hormone," is released in response to stress. Chronic elevation of cortisol levels can have detrimental effects on physical and mental health, contributing to conditions like anxiety, depression, and even cognitive decline.

Physical activity, however, can be a potent tool in managing cortisol levels. Regular exercise can lead to a reduction in baseline cortisol levels, effectively lowering the body's stress response. This decrease in cortisol levels can translate into a calmer overall demeanor, helping to buffer against the harmful effects of chronic stress.

Enhancing Stress Resilience:

Think of physical activity as a training ground for stress resilience. When you exercise regularly, you expose your body to controlled stressors, helping it become more adept at managing and recovering from stress. Over time, this practice can lead to a more adaptive stress response.

Exercise not only strengthens your muscles but also your ability to handle life's challenges. It's a way to fortify your mental armor, making you more resistant to the wear and tear of stress.

The Mind-Body Connection:

The connection between stress reduction and physical activity is not just a physiological one; it's deeply rooted in the mind-body connection. When you exercise, you experience a sense of mastery and control over your body and your environment. This sense of control can be empowering, helping to reduce feelings of helplessness and anxiety that often accompany stress.

Moreover, physical activity promotes the release of endorphins—the body's natural painkillers and mood elevators. These endorphins create a sense of well-being and can counteract the negative emotional effects of stress.

A Respite from the Daily Grind:

In a world where stressors abound, physical activity becomes a sanctuary—a respite from the daily grind. It's a time when you can step away from your worries and focus on the present moment. It's a moment of self-care, where the stresses of life take a back seat to the rhythm of your movements.

Soothing the Mind for Sounder Sleep:

Quality sleep is the body's way of recharging, rejuvenating, and maintaining overall health. However, many individuals, especially those facing mental health challenges, struggle with sleep disturbances like insomnia or restless nights.

Enter exercise as a natural remedy. Engaging in physical activity can help regulate sleep patterns and improve the quality of your slumber. Here's how:

1. Regulating Circadian Rhythms: Our bodies operate on a natural clock, known as the circadian rhythm, which influences our sleep-wake cycle. Physical activity, especially when exposed to natural light, can help synchronize this internal clock with the external world. This synchronization makes it easier to fall asleep at night and wake up refreshed in the morning.

2. Releasing Tension: Anxiety, stress, and physical tension often accompany sleep disturbances. Exercise can serve as a powerful outlet for releasing pent-up tension, promoting a sense of relaxation conducive to sleep.

3. Calming the Mind: Exercise also stimulates the release of endorphins, the body's natural mood elevators. This endorphin release can have a calming effect on the mind, helping to reduce racing thoughts and anxiety that may interfere with sleep.

4. Temperature Regulation: Physical activity can raise body temperature, and the subsequent drop in temperature after exercise can signal to the body that it's time to sleep. This drop in temperature is a natural part of the body's sleep-wake cycle.

Reducing Anxiety's Grip:

Anxiety is a formidable adversary that can overshadow the joy and serenity of life. Physical activity, however, is a potent tool for reducing the grip of anxiety and regaining control over your emotional state.

1. Releasing Feel-Good Neurotransmitters: Engaging in exercise triggers the release of dopamine and serotonin—neurotransmitters associated with feelings of pleasure, reward, and well-being. These neurotransmitters can counteract the negative effects of anxiety, creating a more positive mood.

2. Lowering Cortisol Levels: As mentioned earlier, exercise can help lower cortisol levels—the body's primary stress hormone. By reducing cortisol, exercise can mitigate the physiological effects of anxiety, such as a racing heart and tense muscles.

3. Distraction and Mindfulness: Exercise can serve as a healthy distraction from anxious thoughts. The focus required for physical activity can shift your attention away from worries, promoting mindfulness and presence in the moment.

4. Enhancing Resilience: Regular exercise can boost your overall resilience to stress and anxiety. It's like building a strong fortress against the tumultuous winds of life's challenges.

A Holistic Approach to Mental Health:

Physical activity is a holistic approach to mental health, addressing sleep and anxiety with remarkable efficacy. It is a reminder that our bodies and minds are intricately linked, and positive changes in one domain can ripple through to the other.

As you continue your journey into the mental health-physical activity connection, consider the transformative potential of exercise in both sleep and anxiety management. It's a tool that empowers you to reclaim restful nights and regain control over your emotional state, guiding you toward a path of improved mental well-being.

Chapter 3: Personal Stories of Transformation

Real-life Accounts of Individuals Who Found Solace in Physical Activity

In the chapters that have unfolded thus far, we've explored the scientific underpinnings of the mental health-physical activity connection. Now, as we delve into Chapter 3, we shift our focus to the human aspect of this journey—the stories of real individuals who have discovered solace, strength, and transformation through the embrace of physical activity.

Sarah's Journey from Anxiety to Empowerment:

Sarah's story is a testament to the healing power of physical activity in the face of anxiety. She recounts how, for years, anxiety had kept her in its suffocating grip. She lived with constant worry, her mind racing with worst-case scenarios. Anxiety had become her unwelcome companion, dictating the terms of her life.

But one day, in a moment of determination, Sarah decided to confront her anxiety head-on. She started by taking daily walks in her neighborhood. The simple act of walking, surrounded by nature's beauty, allowed her to slow down and breathe. Gradually, she ventured into more structured forms of exercise, such as yoga and swimming.

Through her consistent efforts, Sarah discovered that exercise provided a respite from her anxious thoughts. It allowed her to experience moments of calm and tranquility that had eluded her for years. As she continued her journey, she also found a supportive community of like-minded individuals in her fitness classes, offering not only companionship but also a sense of belonging she had longed for.

Sarah's story is a poignant reminder that physical activity can be a lifeline for those battling anxiety, offering a path to empowerment, emotional balance, and a life not defined by fear.

James' Triumph Over Depression through Running:

James' life had been marked by the persistent shadow of depression. The weight of sadness seemed insurmountable, making even the simplest daily tasks feel like monumental challenges. His journey with depression was a long and arduous one, marked by periods of isolation and despair.

Then, one day, a glimmer of hope appeared in the form of running. James decided to lace up his sneakers and take his first steps on a local running trail. It was not an easy start, as depression still whispered doubts and insecurities in his ear. But he persisted, setting small goals and gradually increasing his mileage.

With each run, James felt a subtle shift in his mood. The rhythmic pounding of his feet on the pavement became a meditation of sorts, quieting the incessant chatter of depression. The sense of accomplishment he gained from hitting milestones in his running journey bolstered his self-esteem, counteracting the feelings of worthlessness that had plagued him.

Over time, running became James' therapy—a way to process his emotions, release pent-up stress, and build resilience. The endorphins he experienced after a run became a ray of light in the darkness of depression.

James' story is a testament to the transformative potential of physical activity in the face of even the most persistent mental health challenges. It shows us that with determination and the right support, it is possible to break free from the clutches of depression and rediscover the joy of living.

Laura's Journey to Self-Love Through Dance:

Laura had spent much of her life grappling with low self-esteem and a negative body image. She had always felt like an outsider, constantly comparing herself to others and feeling inadequate. The idea of engaging in physical activity seemed daunting, as it brought with it a fear of judgment and ridicule.

However, Laura's perspective shifted when she discovered the world of dance. She joined a dance class that focused on self-expression rather than perfection. It was a place where she could move freely and connect with her body without judgment.

Dance became Laura's sanctuary—a space where she could express her emotions, release pent-up frustrations, and celebrate her body's abilities. With each graceful movement, she learned to appreciate her body for what it could do rather than how it appeared. The supportive community of dancers welcomed her with open arms, reinforcing her sense of belonging.

Through dance, Laura began to cultivate self-love and self-acceptance. She realized that physical activity wasn't about conforming to societal standards; it was about embracing and celebrating her unique self. Her journey taught her that physical activity could be a means of healing not just the body but also the soul.

These are just a few of the many stories that illuminate the transformative power of physical activity in the realm of mental health. As we continue our journey, let these stories serve as beacons of hope and inspiration, reminding us that no matter where we are on our own path, there is solace and strength to be found in the embrace of physical activity.

Emily's Triumph Over Depression:

Emily's journey through the fog of depression was a daunting one. She found herself trapped in a cycle of hopelessness, unable to see a way out. The world felt gray, and even the simplest tasks seemed insurmountable.

But Emily's turning point came when she discovered the therapeutic power of exercise. She started with small steps, quite literally, by going for short walks in her local park. These walks offered her a brief respite from the suffocating grip of depression.

As she continued, Emily began to incorporate more vigorous forms of exercise into her routine. She joined a local gym and attended group fitness classes. The camaraderie and support of the class members became a vital part of her journey.

Through months of consistent effort, Emily felt a profound shift. The release of endorphins during exercise lifted her mood, providing moments of clarity and hope amidst the darkness. She found that setting and achieving fitness goals gave her a sense of purpose and accomplishment that had been missing in her life.

Over time, Emily's depression began to loosen its grip. Exercise became her anchor—a source of strength and resilience. It allowed her to regain control of her life and rediscover the beauty in the world.

Emily's story reminds us that even in the depths of depression, there is a glimmer of hope. Physical activity can be a lifeline, offering a path to recovery and emotional well-being.

Alex's Journey from Anxiety to Confidence:

Alex had lived with crippling anxiety for as long as he could remember. Social situations filled him with dread, and self-doubt was a constant companion. He felt like he was missing out on life's opportunities because of his anxiety.

One day, inspired by a friend's suggestion, Alex decided to try martial arts. Stepping into the dojo was a nerve-wracking experience, but he was determined to confront his anxiety head-on.

As he began his martial arts training, Alex discovered that the discipline and focus required in martial arts provided a sense of control over his anxiety. The structured nature of the practice helped him gain confidence in his abilities.

Through consistent training, Alex started to notice changes not only in his physical strength but also in his mental resilience. Martial arts taught him to confront challenges with a calm and focused mind. The supportive community of fellow practitioners became a source of encouragement and camaraderie.

Over time, Alex's anxiety began to lose its hold on him. He found that the skills he had developed in martial arts—self-discipline, mindfulness, and self-assuredness—extended to other aspects of his life. He was no longer held back by anxiety but empowered by his newfound confidence.

Alex's journey exemplifies how physical activity can be a powerful tool for individuals battling anxiety. It offers not only physical strength but also a profound sense of self-assurance and the ability to face life's challenges with resilience.

Michelle's Transformation Through Yoga:

Michelle's life had been marked by chronic anxiety and panic attacks. She felt like she was constantly on edge, unable to find peace within herself. Traditional forms of exercise had always felt intimidating, so she decided to explore a gentler path—yoga.

Yoga introduced Michelle to the practice of mindfulness and deep breathing. Through each pose and breath, she learned to connect with her body and find stillness in her mind. It was a revelation—a way to calm the storm of anxiety that had raged within her for so long.

With time, Michelle's yoga practice became a sanctuary—a place where she could release the tension and anxious thoughts that had plagued her. She found that yoga offered not just physical flexibility but also emotional flexibility. It allowed her to navigate life's challenges with a sense of serenity and acceptance.

Through yoga, Michelle discovered a path to self-compassion. She learned to be kind to herself and let go of the relentless self-criticism that had fueled her anxiety. The supportive yoga community provided her with a sense of belonging and connection that had been missing in her life.

Michelle's story illustrates the gentler side of physical activity, demonstrating that even low-impact practices like yoga can be potent tools for overcoming anxiety. It offers a reminder that the journey to mental well-being can take many forms, and there is a path that resonates with each individual.

These stories exemplify the profound transformation that physical activity can facilitate in the lives of those grappling with depression and anxiety. They serve as beacons of hope, showing that with determination, support, and the right form of exercise, it is possible to triumph over the most formidable mental health challenges.

David's Journey to Self-assuredness through Weightlifting:

David had struggled with self-esteem issues for much of his life. He felt overshadowed by self-doubt, which had a profound impact on his personal and professional life. But David's life took a transformative turn when he ventured into the world of weightlifting.

As he began lifting weights, David discovered a newfound sense of strength—both physical and emotional. The incremental progress he made in the gym translated into tangible achievements in his life. Each additional pound he could lift became a symbol of his growing self-confidence.

Weightlifting also introduced David to the concept of setting and achieving goals. He found that as he set targets for his workouts and steadily surpassed them, he developed a deep sense of accomplishment. This sense of accomplishment extended beyond the gym, giving him the confidence to tackle challenges in other aspects of his life.

With time, David's physical strength became a metaphor for his inner strength. The discipline and dedication he cultivated through weightlifting empowered him to face life's obstacles with newfound assurance. He no longer felt weighed down by self-doubt but lifted by self-assuredness.

David's journey illustrates the transformative potential of physical activity in bolstering self-esteem. Weightlifting, in particular, can provide a tangible sense of achievement and personal growth, empowering individuals to believe in their own capabilities.

Sara's Empowerment through Martial Arts:

Sara had always felt like she was in the shadows, overshadowed by others' opinions and expectations. Her self-esteem had suffered as a result, and she yearned for a way to reclaim her sense of self. It was then that she discovered martial arts.

Martial arts introduced Sara to a world where she could cultivate her physical and mental strength. As she progressed through the ranks and honed her skills, she realized that she was capable of far more than she had ever imagined. Her confidence grew with each technique she mastered.

Moreover, martial arts instilled in Sara a sense of discipline and resilience. The challenging nature of the practice taught her that setbacks were merely opportunities for growth. She learned to face failure with grace and determination, a lesson that extended to her life beyond the dojo.

Through martial arts, Sara discovered her inner warrior—a source of empowerment and self-assuredness. She was no longer confined by the expectations of others but guided by her own strength and determination.

Sara's journey serves as a powerful reminder that physical activity, particularly martial arts, can be a catalyst for empowerment and self-confidence. It offers individuals a path to discover their inner strength and embrace their uniqueness.

Mark's Transformation through Running:

Mark had always been plagued by self-doubt. He questioned his abilities and often hesitated to take on challenges. But everything changed when he laced up his running shoes and embarked on a journey of self-discovery through running.

Running became Mark's metaphor for life. Each step he took symbolized his forward progress, and each mile he conquered became a testament to his determination. He learned that he could push through physical and mental barriers he had once deemed insurmountable.

With each race he completed, Mark's self-esteem soared. He realized that he was capable of achieving remarkable feats when he set his mind to it. The discipline he cultivated in his running practice extended to other aspects of his life, enabling him to face professional challenges and personal aspirations with unwavering confidence.

Through running, Mark discovered a deep well of self-belief. He was no longer defined by self-doubt but guided by the conviction that he could overcome any obstacle in his path.

Mark's journey underscores the transformative power of running and physical activity in boosting self-esteem. It demonstrates how the pursuit of personal goals and the achievement of milestones can elevate one's sense of self-worth and confidence.

These stories exemplify the profound impact of physical activity in boosting self-esteem and confidence. They serve as inspiration for individuals seeking to harness the transformative potential of exercise to believe in themselves and embrace their unique strengths.

Maria's Journey from Sedentary to Triathlete:

Maria's life had been marked by a sedentary routine and a series of health challenges. She struggled with her weight and had low energy levels, which took a toll on her self-esteem. But Maria's life took an extraordinary turn when she decided to take up triathlon training.

She began with modest goals—short swims, bike rides, and runs. The early days were tough, and Maria faced many physical and mental hurdles. But she was determined to push through. Each day, she took one step closer to her goal of completing a triathlon.

Through her training, Maria discovered a newfound sense of resilience. She learned that she was capable of far more than she had previously believed. Her body grew stronger, and her self-esteem soared as she overcame obstacles in her workouts.

Finally, the day of the triathlon arrived, and Maria completed it with a sense of accomplishment that radiated through her. She had transformed from a sedentary individual into a triathlete—a testament to the power of determination and physical activity. Her story reminds us that it's never too late to embark on a journey of transformation and resilience.

Tom's Recovery from Injury Through Adaptive Sports:

Tom was an avid athlete until a life-altering accident left him with a spinal cord injury. He faced the challenge of adapting to a new reality and redefining his relationship with physical activity. It was through adaptive sports that Tom found a path to recovery and resilience.

He discovered wheelchair basketball, a sport that allowed him to engage in competitive play once again. Tom's journey in adaptive sports was marked by perseverance and an unwavering spirit. He honed his skills, competed at a high level, and even represented his country in international competitions.

Through adaptive sports, Tom not only regained his physical strength but also found renewed purpose and resilience. He showed the world that life-changing events need not define or limit one's potential. Tom's story is a testament to the human spirit's capacity for resilience and adaptation through physical activity.

Lena's Triumph Over Chronic Pain Through Yoga:

Lena's life had been overshadowed by chronic pain and physical limitations. She had tried various treatments, but none had provided lasting relief. It was through the practice of yoga that Lena found a means of managing her pain and experiencing personal change.

Yoga introduced Lena to the concept of mindfulness and pain management. Through gentle movements, deep breathing, and meditation, she learned to connect with her body and alleviate physical discomfort. The practice allowed her to regain a sense of control over her body and life.

As Lena continued her yoga practice, she not only experienced reduced pain but also a profound shift in her mindset. She embraced a more positive outlook and found strength in her newfound resilience. Lena's journey demonstrates the transformative power of physical activity in overcoming physical challenges and fostering personal change.

These stories highlight the extraordinary resilience and change that can emerge through physical activity. They serve as a testament to the indomitable human spirit and the potential for personal transformation, even in the face of adversity.

Chapter 4: Breaking Down the Barriers

Identifying Common Obstacles to Starting an Exercise Routine

Understanding these obstacles is the first step towards overcoming them and embracing the mental health-physical activity connection.

Barrier 1: Lack of Time:

One of the most frequently cited barriers to exercise is the perception of a lack of time. Modern life can be incredibly busy, with work, family responsibilities, and social commitments vying for our attention. The idea of finding an extra hour for exercise can seem daunting.

Barrier 2: Motivation and Consistency:

Many individuals struggle with maintaining the motivation and consistency needed for an exercise routine. The initial burst of enthusiasm can wane over time, leading to a cycle of starting and stopping.

Barrier 3: Fear of Judgment:

The fear of being judged by others can be a powerful deterrent. Some individuals feel self-conscious about their appearance, fitness level, or abilities when they consider joining a gym or participating in group fitness classes.

Barrier 4: Physical Limitations or Health Concerns:

Physical limitations, injuries, or health concerns can create significant barriers to exercise. These limitations may be perceived as insurmountable obstacles, preventing individuals from even attempting physical activity.

Barrier 5: Lack of Knowledge or Guidance:

For some, a lack of knowledge about how to start an exercise routine or the uncertainty about what type of exercise is suitable can be a significant roadblock.

Barrier 6: Financial Constraints:

The cost associated with gym memberships, fitness classes, or specialized equipment can be a limiting factor for many individuals.

Barrier 7: Emotional Barriers:

Emotional challenges, such as anxiety, depression, or a history of trauma, can create substantial barriers to starting an exercise routine. These emotional hurdles can make it difficult to even contemplate engaging in physical activity.

Barrier 8: Social Isolation:

Feelings of social isolation can deter individuals from exercise. Some may not have a support system or workout partner to motivate and encourage them.

Barrier 9: Perfectionism:

The belief that exercise must be done perfectly or at a high level of intensity can lead to inaction. Perfectionism can be paralyzing and prevent individuals from even taking the first step.

Barrier 10: Lack of Enjoyment:

If exercise is not enjoyable or engaging, it becomes challenging to sustain. Many people associate exercise with drudgery, which can discourage them from incorporating it into their lives.

Understanding these common barriers is crucial for anyone seeking to overcome them and embrace the benefits of physical activity for mental health. In the following chapters, we will explore strategies and solutions for breaking down these barriers, making exercise more accessible and achievable for all.

Strategy 1: Start Small and Set Achievable Goals:

Begin with modest goals that are attainable, even on your busiest days. For example, commit to a 10-minute walk each day or doing a few simple stretches. Achieving these small milestones can boost your confidence and set a positive tone for your fitness journey.

Strategy 2: Cultivate a Growth Mindset:

Shift your mindset from a fixed perspective to a growth-oriented one. Understand that progress takes time and setbacks are a part of the process. Embrace challenges as opportunities for growth and learning rather than as failures.

Strategy 3: Find Your Intrinsic Motivation:

Discover what truly motivates you to exercise. Is it the sense of accomplishment, stress relief, improved mood, or better health? Identifying your intrinsic motivation can help you stay committed even when external factors wane.

Strategy 4: Build a Support System:

Enlist the support of friends, family, or a workout buddy who can provide encouragement, accountability, and companionship. Sharing your fitness journey with others can make it more enjoyable and motivating.

Strategy 5: Create a Realistic Schedule:

Recognize that time is a valuable resource, and schedule your workouts as appointments in your calendar. Treat exercise as a non-negotiable commitment to yourself, just like any other important task.

Strategy 6: Embrace Variety and Fun:

Explore different forms of physical activity until you find something you genuinely enjoy. Whether it's dancing, hiking, swimming, or team sports, having fun while exercising can make it feel less like a chore.

Strategy 7: Use Positive Self-Talk:

Challenge and replace negative thoughts with positive affirmations. Remind yourself of your accomplishments, no matter how small they may seem, and reinforce your belief in your ability to reach your fitness goals.

Strategy 8: Break It Down Into Manageable Steps:

If the thought of a long workout is overwhelming, break it down into smaller, manageable steps. Tell yourself, "I'll start with five minutes," and then gradually extend the duration as you gain momentum.

Strategy 9: Celebrate Your Progress:

Acknowledge and celebrate your achievements, no matter how minor they may appear. Recognize the positive changes you've experienced in your physical and mental well-being as you continue your fitness journey.

Strategy 10: Seek Professional Guidance:

Consider consulting with a fitness trainer, coach, or mental health professional who specializes in exercise psychology. They can provide tailored strategies and support to address specific self-doubt and inertia challenges.

By implementing these strategies, you can effectively conquer self-doubt and inertia, allowing you to embark on and sustain an exercise routine that promotes not only physical health but also mental well-being.

Tips for Fitting Physical Activity into a Busy Lifestyle

In today's fast-paced world, finding time for physical activity can be challenging. However, it's entirely possible to incorporate exercise into a busy lifestyle with some strategic planning and dedication. Here are some practical tips to help you make physical activity a part of your daily routine:

1. Prioritize Exercise:

Treat physical activity as a non-negotiable appointment in your schedule. Just as you wouldn't skip an important work meeting, prioritize your workouts by setting aside dedicated time for them.

2. Set Realistic Goals:

Establish achievable fitness goals that align with your schedule. Whether it's a short daily workout, a weekend hike, or a weekly fitness class, setting realistic expectations will make it easier to stick with your routine.

3. Incorporate Activity Throughout the Day:

Look for opportunities to add movement to your daily routine. Take the stairs instead of the elevator, walk or bike to work if possible, and use short breaks to stretch or do quick exercises.

4. Make the Most of Your Commute:

If you commute to work, consider walking or biking part of the way. Alternatively, get off public transportation one stop earlier and walk the remaining distance.

5. Use Technology to Your Advantage:

Utilize fitness apps and wearable devices to track your activity and set reminders for workouts. These tools can help you stay accountable and motivated.

6. Involve Your Social Network:

Combine social time with physical activity by inviting friends or family members to join you for a workout or outdoor activity. It's a great way to stay connected while staying active.

7. Break It Up:

You don't need to do one long workout session; shorter bursts of activity throughout the day can be just as effective. Consider doing 10-minute workouts in the morning, during lunch, and in the evening.

8. Multitask Mindfully:

While it's important to focus on your workout, you can still multitask to some extent. Listen to podcasts or audiobooks while walking or jogging, or catch up on work-related calls during a brisk walk.

9. Incorporate Family Time:

Make physical activity a family affair. Go for hikes, bike rides, or play sports together. It's a wonderful way to bond while staying active.

10. Embrace Home Workouts:

If you can't make it to a gym or fitness class, there are numerous home workout programs available online. You can follow along with video workouts that require minimal or no equipment.

11. Plan and Prep Meals:

Spend some time on meal planning and preparation to save time during the week. Having healthy meals readily available can free up time for exercise.

12. Be Flexible:

Life can be unpredictable, so be open to adjusting your workout schedule when necessary. If you miss a session, don't be discouraged; simply reschedule it.

13. Stay Consistent:

Consistency is key. Make exercise a regular part of your routine, and over time, it will become a habit that you won't want to skip.

Remember, the most important aspect of fitting physical activity into a busy lifestyle is finding a routine that works for you and is sustainable in the long term. Start small, stay committed, and gradually build on your efforts to improve your physical and mental well-being.

Creating a Supportive Environment for Success

To effectively integrate physical activity into your life and reap the mental health benefits, it's essential to cultivate a supportive environment that encourages and sustains your efforts. Here are practical steps to create that supportive atmosphere:

1. Set Clear Goals:

Define specific fitness goals that are meaningful to you. Having clear objectives will provide direction and motivation for your journey.

2. Communicate Your Intentions:

Share your fitness goals and plans with close friends, family, or a trusted support network. When others know about your commitment, they can provide encouragement and understanding.

3. Identify Potential Obstacles:

Recognize the obstacles or challenges that may arise on your fitness path. Once you identify them, you can proactively address and overcome them.

4. Plan Your Workouts:

Schedule your workouts in advance and treat them like important appointments. Having a set schedule makes it easier to prioritize exercise in your daily life.

5. Create a Home Workout Space:

If time constraints or other factors make it challenging to visit a gym, set up a dedicated space for home workouts. Even a small area with some basic equipment can suffice.

6. Invest in Comfortable Attire:

Purchase comfortable workout attire and shoes that make you feel good and confident during exercise. Feeling physically comfortable can boost your motivation.

7. Join a Fitness Community:

Consider joining fitness classes or local sports teams to be part of a community that shares your interests. Being around like-minded individuals can provide motivation and a sense of belonging.

8. Hire a Trainer or Coach:

If you're unsure where to start or need personalized guidance, consider working with a fitness trainer or coach. They can create tailored plans and offer support.

9. Keep a Fitness Journal:

Maintain a journal to track your progress, set goals, and reflect on your experiences. This can help you stay accountable and monitor your growth.

10. Incorporate Family and Friends:

Involve your family and friends in your fitness journey by including them in activities or workouts. Shared experiences can strengthen bonds and create a positive environment.

11. Set Up Rewards:

Establish a system of rewards for achieving milestones in your fitness journey. Rewards can serve as powerful incentives to keep you motivated.

12. Educate Yourself:

Learn about the benefits of physical activity for mental health and overall well-being. Understanding the science behind it can reinforce your commitment.

13. Practice Self-Compassion:

Be kind to yourself and acknowledge that setbacks and challenges are a natural part of the process. Avoid self-criticism and focus on self-encouragement.

14. Adapt to Life Changes:

Recognize that life is dynamic, and your fitness routine may need to adapt to changing circumstances. Flexibility is key to long-term success.

15. Seek Professional Guidance:

If you face specific mental health challenges or physical limitations, consider consulting mental health professionals or physical therapists who can provide tailored support.

By creating a supportive environment that aligns with your fitness goals and values, you'll be better equipped to overcome obstacles, stay motivated, and experience the mental health benefits of regular physical activity. Remember that your environment plays a crucial role in shaping your habits, so make it one that fosters your success and well-being.

Chapter 5: Finding Your Why

The Importance of Setting Clear Goals

In this chapter, we'll explore the significance of setting clear and meaningful goals as a foundational step in harnessing the mental health benefits of regular physical activity.

1. Providing Direction and Focus:

Clear goals act as a compass, guiding your fitness journey with a defined direction. When you have a specific target in mind, you know exactly where you're headed and can channel your efforts more effectively.

2. Motivation and Commitment:

Goals serve as powerful motivators. They give you a reason to stay committed to your exercise routine, especially when faced with obstacles or distractions. The pursuit of your goals becomes the driving force behind your dedication.

3. Measuring Progress:

Clear goals provide a benchmark for measuring your progress. By setting milestones and tracking your achievements, you can see how far you've come and gain a sense of accomplishment along the way.

4. Creating Accountability:

When you establish goals, you create a sense of accountability—both to yourself and potentially to others. Sharing your goals with friends, family, or a fitness community can increase your commitment to achieving them.

5. Boosting Confidence and Self-Efficacy:

As you work towards your goals and see your abilities grow, your confidence and self-efficacy (belief in your capability) naturally increase. This newfound confidence extends beyond your fitness journey and can positively impact other areas of your life.

6. Providing Purpose and Meaning:

Clear goals infuse your exercise routine with purpose and meaning. They answer the "why" behind your actions, connecting your fitness journey to your broader life goals and values.

7. Enhancing Mental Health Benefits:

Goals are instrumental in unlocking the mental health benefits of physical activity. When you set goals that align with reducing stress, improving mood, or enhancing overall well-being, you're more likely to experience these benefits.

8. Overcoming Challenges:

Challenges and setbacks are part of any fitness journey. Clear goals provide the resilience needed to overcome these hurdles. They remind you of your purpose and encourage you to persevere.

9. Celebrating Achievements:

Each goal achieved is a cause for celebration. These celebrations not only reinforce your commitment but also boost your motivation to set and conquer new challenges.

10. Creating a Long-Term Habit:

Goals help transform exercise into a long-term habit. By consistently setting and achieving goals, you integrate physical activity into your lifestyle, making it a sustainable practice.

11. Aligning with Your Values:

Your fitness goals should align with your core values and priorities. When they do, your journey becomes more meaningful, and your efforts feel more purposeful.

12. Personalizing Your Path:

Goals are personal. They allow you to tailor your fitness journey to your unique needs and aspirations. Whether your focus is on weight loss, stress reduction, or building strength, your goals shape the path you take.

13. Inspiring Others:

Your pursuit of meaningful fitness goals can inspire those around you. Your commitment and progress may motivate friends and family to embark on their own health and fitness journeys.

In essence, setting clear goals is the foundation upon which you build a successful and rewarding fitness journey. They provide direction, motivation, and a sense of purpose that can elevate not only your physical health but also your mental and emotional well-being. In the chapters that follow, we'll delve into the process of identifying and setting the right goals to unlock the full potential of physical activity for your mental health.

Connecting Your Fitness Journey to Your Mental Health

Imagine waking up on a crisp morning, the sun just beginning to paint the sky with hues of gold and pink. You slip on your running shoes, take a deep breath, and step outside. As your feet hit the pavement, you feel a surge of energy and anticipation. This is your time – a moment to connect with yourself, to clear your mind, and to nurture your mental health.

Goals that Speak to Your Soul

Consider your fitness goals. Are they aligned with what truly matters to you? Are they anchored in your core values? When your fitness goals resonate with your soul, they become more than just objectives; they become a source of inspiration and motivation.

For instance, imagine someone whose goal is to complete a half marathon. It's not just about the race; it's about the sense of accomplishment, the dedication to training, and the opportunity to prove to themselves that they can achieve something extraordinary. This goal is deeply rooted in self-belief and can serve as a powerful catalyst for improved mental health.

The Mental Health Boost

Physical activity has a profound impact on the brain. When you exercise, your body releases endorphins – those magical neurotransmitters that trigger feelings of happiness and euphoria. These endorphins are like a natural mood booster, washing away stress, anxiety, and even symptoms of depression.

But the connection goes beyond the momentary euphoria. Regular physical activity has been linked to long-term improvements in mental health. It can reduce the risk of developing mood disorders, enhance self-esteem, and improve overall cognitive function.

Let's return to our runner. As they lace up their shoes and hit the pavement, they're not just working on their physical fitness; they're investing in their mental well-being. The rhythmic pounding of their feet on the ground becomes a meditation of sorts, quieting the noise in their mind and allowing them to find clarity and focus.

Stress Reduction and Resilience

In our fast-paced, modern lives, stress has become a constant companion. But physical activity is a potent antidote. It helps your body and mind adapt to stress, building resilience and reducing the negative impacts of chronic stress.

Imagine someone whose goal is to master yoga. As they flow through poses and connect with their breath, they're not just improving flexibility and balance; they're learning to manage stress. Yoga teaches them to stay present, to let go of worries, and to embrace serenity. This newfound resilience ripples into their daily life, enabling them to handle stressors with grace and composure.

The Power of Routine

Consistency is the linchpin of any fitness journey. When you commit to regular physical activity, you're not only improving your physical health but also establishing a routine that fosters mental well-being.

Think of someone who sets a goal to meditate for ten minutes every morning. As they sit in quiet contemplation, they're not just calming their mind in that moment; they're creating a daily ritual of self-care. This routine becomes a sanctuary, a space for reflection and self-compassion that can significantly improve their mental health over time.

A Sense of Control

Life often throws unexpected challenges our way. But a well-structured fitness goal can provide a sense of control, especially in uncertain times.

Consider someone who takes up strength training. As they progressively increase their weights and master new exercises, they're not just building physical strength; they're cultivating a sense of control over their body and life. This empowerment spills over into other aspects of their existence, reminding them that they have the strength to overcome obstacles, both physical and mental.

Mind-Body Harmony

Physical activity isn't just about the body; it's about the mind-body connection. It's about discovering the synergy between your physical and mental well-being.

Imagine someone who practices tai chi, a graceful martial art that emphasizes mindfulness and flowing movements. As they move through the forms, they're not just honing balance and coordination; they're finding harmony between body and mind. This harmonious connection fosters a deep sense of tranquility and self-awareness, benefiting their mental health immensely.

Your Unique Fitness Journey

Your fitness journey is as unique as your fingerprint. It's an exploration of your strengths and a journey toward your potential. But it's also a pathway to mental health, a means of nurturing your emotional well-being, and a source of resilience in the face of life's challenges.

So, as you set your fitness goals, remember that they're not just about physical achievements. They're about the joy of movement, the celebration of progress, and the empowerment of your mind. Your fitness journey is a testament to your inner strength and a testament to the profound connection between your physical and mental health.

Strategies for Maintaining Motivation

Imagine a ship navigating a vast ocean. The wind in its sails represents your motivation, propelling you forward on your fitness journey. But like the wind, motivation can change direction and intensity. To keep your ship on course, you must become a skilled navigator of your own motivation.

1. Cultivate Intrinsic Motivation:

Intrinsic motivation, driven by internal factors like personal satisfaction and enjoyment, is a powerful force. Connect your fitness goals to activities you genuinely love, as this intrinsic motivation will be more enduring than external rewards or pressures.

2. Set Meaningful Goals:

Ensure that your fitness goals resonate with your core values and desires. When your goals align with what truly matters to you, they become a constant source of motivation and purpose.

3. Create a Vision Board:

Visualize your goals by creating a vision board. This collage of images and words can serve as a daily reminder of what you're working towards, kindling your motivation each time you see it.

4. Break It Down:

Large, daunting goals can feel overwhelming. Break them into smaller, manageable milestones. Celebrating these mini-achievements along the way provides regular boosts of motivation.

5. Find an Accountability Partner:

Share your goals with a friend, family member, or workout buddy. Having someone to check in with can increase your commitment and motivation.

6. Track Your Progress:

Maintain a record of your fitness journey. Tracking your progress, whether through a journal, app, or spreadsheet, can be a powerful motivator as you witness your growth over time.

7. Embrace Variety:

Monotony can drain motivation. Keep things fresh by incorporating various activities and workouts into your routine. Variety not only prevents boredom but also challenges your body and mind in new ways.

8. Join a Fitness Community:

Engage with a fitness community or group, either online or in-person. The camaraderie and shared experiences can provide valuable motivation and support.

9. Visualize Success:

Take a moment each day to visualize your success. Imagine how achieving your goals will make you feel and the positive impact it will have on your mental health.

10. Utilize Positive Self-Talk:

Replace negative thoughts with positive affirmations. Encourage yourself with kind and motivating self-talk, especially during challenging moments.

11. Reward Yourself:

Establish a system of rewards for reaching specific milestones. These rewards can serve as motivation and make the journey more enjoyable.

12. Create a Consistent Routine:

Habitual actions require less conscious effort. Establish a regular exercise routine, making physical activity an integral part of your daily life.

13. Seek Inspiration:

Read books, watch documentaries, or follow fitness influencers who inspire you. Their stories and achievements can fuel your motivation and determination.

14. Stay Mindful of Your "Why":

Regularly revisit the reasons why you embarked on this fitness journey in the first place. Reconnecting with your "why" can reignite your motivation.

15. Be Patient and Kind to Yourself:

Motivation can ebb and flow. Understand that there will be days when motivation is low. On those days, be gentle with yourself and take small steps to keep moving forward.

Your fitness journey is a dynamic voyage, and motivation is your ever-changing wind. By implementing these strategies, you can steer your ship even when the winds are calm or challenging. Remember that motivation is not a constant; it's a skill you can nurture and cultivate throughout your journey toward improved mental health through physical activity.

Defining Your Unique Reasons for Getting Active

Imagine standing at the edge of a dense forest. The path before you is shrouded in mystery, but you're filled with anticipation and purpose. You're not here by chance; you're here because you've defined your unique reasons for getting active, and this forest represents the uncharted territory of your fitness journey.

The Quest for Your "Why"

Your "why" is the heart and soul of your fitness journey. It's the compass that points you in the right direction when the path ahead seems unclear. To uncover your unique reasons for getting active, consider these reflective steps:

1. Self-Reflection:

Set aside quiet time for self-reflection. Ask yourself why you want to embark on a fitness journey. What aspects of your mental health and well-being are you seeking to enhance?

2. Identify Your Values:

Think about your core values and what truly matters to you. Your fitness goals should align with these values, giving your journey a sense of purpose and meaning.

3. Explore Your Passions:

Consider your passions and interests. What physical activities ignite your enthusiasm? Connecting your fitness journey to activities you love can infuse it with natural motivation.

4. Visualize Your Ideal Self:

Imagine your ideal self in terms of physical and mental health. How does this vision differ from your current state? Visualizing your future self can clarify your "why."

5. Analyze Pain Points:

Examine areas of your life where you experience mental health challenges or dissatisfaction. How might physical activity alleviate or address these issues?

6. Set Emotional Goals:

Your fitness goals can extend beyond the physical realm. Set emotional goals like reducing stress, increasing confidence, or finding inner peace.

7. Consider the Bigger Picture:

Think about how improved mental health through physical activity can impact your life as a whole. How might it enhance your relationships, work, or overall happiness?

8. Connect to Your Life Narrative:

Your life is a story, and your fitness journey can be a transformative chapter. How does physical activity fit into your narrative, and how can it lead to personal growth and evolution?

Examples of Unique "Whys"

Let's explore some unique "whys" that individuals have discovered on their fitness journeys:

Lucy's Quest for Serenity:

Lucy's life was a whirlwind of responsibilities, leaving her feeling constantly stressed and overwhelmed. Her "why" was to find moments of serenity in her day through yoga. She sought the calmness that yoga could offer, allowing her to better manage stress and regain a sense of balance.

David's Journey to Self-Discovery:

David had always struggled with self-esteem and self-identity. His "why" was to discover his true self through outdoor adventures. Hiking and backpacking gave him a chance to connect with nature and, in the process, connect with himself. His fitness journey became a quest for self-discovery and self-acceptance.

Maria's Mission to Empower Others:

Maria's life had been marked by a series of health challenges. Her "why" was not just about her own well-being but about empowering others. She became a fitness trainer, helping individuals overcome their physical and mental hurdles. Her journey was driven by the desire to make a positive impact on the lives of those she coached.

Connecting to Your "Why"

Your unique "why" is your North Star, guiding you through the forest of your fitness journey. It's what makes your journey uniquely yours and gives you a reason to take each step, even when the path is steep or unclear.

As you define your "why," remember that it's not set in stone. It may evolve and change as you progress on your fitness journey. What's important is that it resonates with your heart and soul, and it becomes the driving force behind your commitment to improving your mental health through physical activity.

Your "why" is your compass, and it will lead you to the transformative benefits of this journey.

Chapter 6: Getting Started: Choosing the Right Activities

Different Forms of Physical Activity (e.g., Walking, Yoga, Weightlifting)

Imagine walking into a vast garden, each path leading to a different experience. Similarly, the world of physical activity offers a multitude of paths, each with its own set of benefits for your mental health. Let's explore some of the diverse forms of physical activity to help you find the one that resonates with you.

1. Walking:

Walking is the simplest and most accessible form of physical activity. Whether it's a leisurely stroll in the park or a brisk walk around your neighborhood, walking can be a gentle yet effective way to improve your mood, reduce stress, and clear your mind. The rhythmic motion of walking can be meditative, allowing you to connect with your thoughts and emotions.

2. Yoga:

Yoga is a holistic practice that combines physical postures, breath control, and mindfulness. It promotes relaxation, reduces anxiety, and improves flexibility and balance. Yoga's emphasis on mindfulness can help you stay present and cultivate a sense of inner peace, making it a valuable tool for mental well-being.

3. Swimming:

Swimming offers a low-impact, full-body workout. The soothing nature of water can have a calming effect on the mind, reducing symptoms of anxiety and depression. It's an excellent choice if you seek a form of physical activity that allows you to disconnect from the outside world and find tranquility in the water.

4. Running or Jogging:

Running or jogging can be an invigorating way to boost your mood and build mental resilience. The release of endorphins during a run can create a "runner's high," promoting a sense of euphoria and stress relief. Additionally, the discipline of setting and achieving running goals can enhance self-esteem.

5. Dance:

Dancing combines physical activity with self-expression and creativity. Whether you prefer ballroom, salsa, hip-hop, or ballet, dancing can be a joyful way to improve your mental health. Dancing releases endorphins, reduces stress, and fosters a sense of connection with your body and others.

6. Weightlifting or Strength Training:

Strength training not only builds physical strength but also enhances mental resilience. Lifting weights can boost self-confidence and provide a sense of accomplishment as you set and achieve strength goals. The discipline and focus required can translate into improved mental well-being.

7. Cycling:

Cycling offers both physical and mental benefits. It's an excellent cardiovascular workout that can improve mood and reduce stress. The sensation of freedom while cycling outdoors or the meditative quality of indoor cycling can be therapeutic for your mental health.

8. Martial Arts:

Martial arts, such as karate, taekwondo, or Brazilian jiu-jitsu, combine physical activity with mental discipline and self-control. These practices can help you build resilience, self-confidence, and a strong sense of self, fostering improved mental well-being.

9. Team Sports:

Participating in team sports like soccer, basketball, or volleyball can enhance your mental health through social connection, teamwork, and the joy of competition. The camaraderie of being part of a team can provide a sense of belonging and support.

10. Hiking and Nature Walks:

Exploring the great outdoors through hiking or nature walks can have a profound impact on mental well-being. Immersing yourself in nature reduces stress, boosts mood, and enhances your connection to the natural world, fostering a sense of tranquility and awe.

Choosing Your Path

Each form of physical activity offers its unique blend of physical and mental health benefits. The key is to choose the one that resonates with you, aligns with your goals, and brings you joy. Your fitness journey is a personal exploration, and the path you choose should reflect your preferences and needs.

Whether you find solace in the stillness of yoga, the exhilaration of running, or the camaraderie of team sports, remember that the most important aspect is to engage in physical activity consistently. It's this commitment that will unlock the mental health benefits, transforming your fitness journey into a path toward improved well-being and resilience.

Assessing Your Fitness Level and Interests

Imagine you're preparing for a grand adventure. To embark on this journey, you need to know where you stand and what excites you. Similarly, beginning a fitness journey requires a self-assessment to determine your starting point and discover what activities resonate with you.

1. Self-Assessment of Fitness Level:

Begin by evaluating your current fitness level. This assessment helps you understand your strengths and areas that may need improvement. Here's how to get started:

◇ **Cardiovascular Fitness:** Assess your endurance by gauging how long you can sustain activities like brisk walking or jogging without feeling fatigued.

◇ **Strength and Muscular Endurance:** Measure your strength through basic bodyweight exercises like push-ups, squats, or planks. Note how many repetitions you can perform with proper form.

◇ **Flexibility:** Determine your flexibility by attempting stretches and yoga poses. Pay attention to areas of tightness or discomfort.

◇ **Balance and Coordination:** Assess your balance by standing on one foot or trying simple balance exercises. Evaluate your coordination through activities like catching or throwing a ball.

2. Setting Realistic Goals:

Based on your fitness assessment, set realistic goals that reflect your current abilities. Setting attainable objectives will prevent discouragement and build confidence as you progress.

◇ If your cardiovascular fitness is low, a realistic goal might be to walk for 20 minutes without stopping within a month.

◇ If your strength is limited, aim to perform a set number of bodyweight exercises, increasing repetitions as you improve.

◇ If flexibility is a challenge, work on stretching exercises to increase your range of motion gradually.

◇ For balance and coordination, set goals to enhance stability through balance exercises and agility drills.

3. Identify Your Interests:

Physical activity should be enjoyable to keep you motivated. Reflect on your interests and passions, as they can guide your choices. Ask yourself:

◇ Do you enjoy being outdoors or prefer indoor activities?

◇ Are you drawn to solo activities that allow for introspection, or do you thrive in social settings and group dynamics?

◇ Are you interested in competitive sports, or do you prefer non-competitive, leisurely pursuits?

◈ Do you find relaxation in mind-body practices like yoga and tai chi, or are you more inclined toward high-energy activities like dancing and aerobics?

4. Experiment and Explore:

Don't be afraid to try different activities. Exploring various options can help you discover what resonates with you the most. Attend fitness classes, engage in short trial sessions, or experiment with different sports and workouts.

5. Seek Professional Guidance:

Consider consulting with a fitness professional or personal trainer. They can provide an individualized assessment, recommend suitable activities, and help you create a tailored fitness plan.

6. Listen to Your Body:

Pay close attention to your body's signals during and after physical activity. Are you experiencing pain or discomfort? Are you feeling invigorated and satisfied? Your body's feedback can guide your choices and ensure your safety.

7. Adapt and Progress:

As you engage in physical activity regularly, your fitness level will improve. Be open to adjusting your goals and trying new activities as you progress. What once seemed challenging may become your new comfort zone.

8. Enjoy the Journey:

Remember that your fitness journey is a process, not a destination. Embrace the ups and downs, and find joy in the small victories along the way. Celebrate your progress and the positive impact on your mental health.

Choosing the Right Fit

By assessing your fitness level and interests, you'll be better equipped to choose activities that align with your capabilities and preferences. The journey to improved mental health through physical activity is a personal adventure, and the path you select should resonate with you on a deep level.

Tailoring Exercise to Your Mental Health Goals

Picture a tailor carefully crafting a suit to fit your body perfectly. Similarly, you can tailor your exercise routine to suit your mental health goals precisely. To do this effectively, follow these steps:

1. Identify Your Mental Health Goals:

Begin by clearly defining your mental health objectives. What specific improvements are you seeking? Common goals include reducing stress, alleviating symptoms of anxiety or depression, boosting self-esteem, enhancing mood, and promoting overall well-being.

2. Understand How Exercise Impacts Mental Health:

Different forms of physical activity can have varying effects on mental health. For example, aerobic exercises like running and swimming are known to boost mood and reduce symptoms of depression. Mind-body practices such as yoga and tai chi emphasize relaxation and stress reduction. Strength training can improve self-esteem and body image. Understanding these impacts can help you choose the right activities.

3. Match Activities to Your Goals:

Select physical activities that align with your mental health goals:

◈ If your goal is stress reduction, consider practices like yoga, meditation, or nature walks.

◈ For mood improvement, aerobic exercises like dancing, cycling, or group fitness classes can be effective.

◈ To enhance self-esteem and body image, strength training and functional fitness workouts may be beneficial.

◈ If you aim to alleviate symptoms of anxiety, mind-body practices like deep breathing exercises, tai chi, or Pilates can be helpful.

4. Integrate Mindfulness and Meditation:

Incorporate mindfulness and meditation into your exercise routine, regardless of the activity you choose. These practices can enhance the mental health benefits of physical activity by promoting present-moment awareness, reducing stress, and fostering a positive mindset.

5. Set SMART Goals:

Create SMART (Specific, Measurable, Achievable, Relevant, Time-bound) goals tailored to your mental health objectives. For example, if your goal is to reduce stress, set a specific target such as practicing yoga for 20 minutes daily for the next three months.

6. Establish a Routine:

Consistency is key to achieving mental health goals through physical activity. Develop a regular exercise routine that fits into your schedule and lifestyle. Consistent practice enhances the cumulative benefits of exercise on your mental well-being.

7. Monitor Progress and Adjust:

Regularly assess your progress toward your mental health goals. If you're not experiencing the desired improvements, be open to adjusting your exercise routine. This may involve trying different activities or intensities or seeking guidance from a fitness professional.

8. Listen to Your Body:

Pay attention to your body's signals during exercise. If you're feeling overwhelmed or fatigued, it's essential to modify your routine or take a break. Pushing too hard can lead to burnout and may not serve your mental health goals.

9. Seek Support and Accountability:

Consider involving a friend, family member, or mental health professional in your journey. They can provide support, encouragement, and accountability, increasing your chances of success.

10. Enjoy the Process:

Lastly, remember to enjoy the process. While achieving your mental health goals is essential, finding joy and fulfillment in your chosen activities will make your fitness journey more sustainable and rewarding.

Tailoring for Transformation

By tailoring your exercise routine to your mental health goals, you can maximize the positive impact physical activity has on your well-being. Just as a finely tailored suit enhances your appearance, a customized exercise plan can enhance your mental health, fostering positive changes that resonate deeply with your unique needs and aspirations.

The Benefits of Variety in Your Routine

Imagine a palette of vibrant colors, each representing a different form of physical activity. Just as an artist uses various hues to create a masterpiece, you can use a variety of exercises to craft a fulfilling fitness routine. Here are the benefits of introducing diversity into your regimen:

1. Preventing Boredom:

Repetitive workouts can become monotonous, leading to boredom and decreased motivation. Variety keeps your fitness routine fresh and exciting, reducing the risk of burnout.

2. Targeting Different Muscle Groups:

Different activities engage various muscle groups. By incorporating a variety of exercises, you ensure a balanced, full-body workout. This not only improves physical fitness but also promotes mental well-being by preventing muscle imbalances and overuse injuries.

3. Mental Stimulation:

Learning and mastering new activities provide mental stimulation. It challenges your brain, improving cognitive function and boosting mood. Variety can be as mentally rewarding as it is physically.

4. Reducing Plateaus:

The body adapts to routine quickly, leading to fitness plateaus. Introducing new exercises or changing the intensity of your workouts challenges your body and allows for continued progress, enhancing self-esteem and motivation.

5. Exploring Interests:

Variety allows you to explore different physical activities and discover what truly resonates with you. You may find unexpected passions or hobbies that become integral to your well-being.

6. Cross-Training Benefits:

Cross-training involves alternating between different types of exercise. For example, combining strength training with aerobic activities like cycling or swimming can provide comprehensive mental health benefits. Cross-training helps prevent overuse injuries, reduces the risk of burnout, and promotes overall fitness.

7. Enhancing Social Connection:

Participating in a variety of activities can expand your social circle. Engaging in group fitness classes, sports, or recreational activities can lead to new friendships and a sense of community, bolstering your mental well-being.

8. Tailoring to Your Mood:

Different activities can address specific emotional needs. For instance, when you need relaxation and stress reduction, you might opt for yoga. When you seek an energy boost, a lively dance class may be more appealing. Having a range of options allows you to tailor your exercise to your mood.

9. Long-Term Sustainability:

Variety promotes long-term adherence to your fitness routine. When you enjoy a diverse set of activities, you're more likely to view exercise as a pleasurable part of your lifestyle rather than a chore.

10. Preventing Exercise Plateaus:

By changing your exercise routine regularly, you can prevent plateaus in both physical and mental progress. Your body and mind continue to adapt, and you can consistently experience the mental health benefits of physical activity.

Sample Variety:

Consider how a week of diverse physical activity might look:

- ◇ Monday: Yoga for relaxation and stress reduction.

- ◇ Tuesday: High-intensity interval training (HIIT) for an energy boost.

- ◇ Wednesday: A nature hike to connect with the outdoors.

- ◇ Thursday: Strength training to build self-esteem and confidence.

- ◇ Friday: Dancing with friends for social interaction and fun.

- ◇ Saturday: Swimming for both physical and mental relaxation.

- ◇ Sunday: A leisurely bike ride to enjoy a change of pace.

Creating Your Mosaic of Wellness

Imagine your fitness routine as a mosaic, with each activity representing a unique piece that contributes to your overall well-being. By embracing variety, you can craft a beautiful mosaic of physical and mental health, ensuring a dynamic and fulfilling fitness journey.

Chapter 7: Establishing a Sustainable Routine

Setting Up a Structured Workout Schedule

Imagine a well-constructed bridge spanning a turbulent river. Just as the bridge provides a reliable path, a structured workout schedule forms the foundation of your fitness journey. It ensures consistency and helps you navigate the ebbs and flows of life while staying on course toward your mental health objectives. Here's how to set up an effective workout schedule:

1. Assess Your Time Availability:

Begin by examining your daily and weekly schedule. Identify time slots when you can commit to physical activity. Consider both weekdays and weekends, as well as morning, afternoon, and evening options.

2. Prioritize Consistency:

Consistency is key to reaping the mental health benefits of physical activity. Aim for regular workouts, even if they're shorter in duration. Consistency trumps sporadic intense sessions.

3. Be Realistic:

Set achievable exercise frequency and duration. It's better to start with a manageable schedule that you can maintain over the long term than to overcommit and risk burnout.

4. Set Specific Goals:

Align your workout schedule with your mental health goals. If stress reduction is your aim, consider scheduling calming activities like yoga or meditation on stressful days.

5. Mix It Up:

Incorporate variety into your schedule. Include different types of exercises to engage various muscle groups and maintain mental stimulation.

6. Create a Weekly Plan:

Outline your exercise plan for the entire week. Assign specific activities to each day, noting the duration and intensity. This provides a clear roadmap for your fitness journey.

7. Include Rest Days:

Rest days are essential for recovery. Integrate rest days into your schedule to allow your body and mind to recuperate. These days can be as beneficial as active ones for your mental health.

8. Adapt to Your Circumstances:

Life is dynamic, and circumstances may change. Be flexible and willing to adapt your schedule when unexpected events or obligations arise.

9. Listen to Your Body:

Pay attention to your body's signals. If you're fatigued or not feeling well, consider adjusting your schedule or choosing a lighter activity for that day.

10. Plan for Progression:

As your fitness level improves, adjust your schedule to accommodate more challenging workouts or longer durations. Progression keeps your fitness journey engaging and motivating.

11. Use Technology and Apps:

Utilize fitness apps and devices to track your workouts and schedule. These tools can help you stay organized and motivated.

12. Seek Accountability:

Tell a friend or family member about your workout schedule. Having someone to check in with can provide accountability and encouragement.

Sample Weekly Schedule:

Here's an example of a structured weekly workout schedule tailored to mental health goals:

⬦ Monday: Yoga for relaxation (30 minutes).

⬦ Tuesday: HIIT for an energy boost (20 minutes).

⬦ Wednesday: Strength training (40 minutes).

⬦ Thursday: Nature walk (45 minutes).

⬦ Friday: Dance class for fun and social interaction (60 minutes).

⬦ Saturday: Swimming for relaxation (30 minutes).

⬦ Sunday: Rest day.

Establishing Routine for Well-Being

A structured workout schedule is the backbone of your fitness journey, guiding you toward your mental health goals. By setting clear objectives, being realistic, and adapting to life's changes, you can establish a routine that not only supports your well-being but also becomes an integral part of your lifestyle.

Building Gradual Progress and Avoiding Burnout

Imagine constructing a magnificent skyscraper. The process requires meticulous planning and a strong foundation to avoid collapse. Similarly, building gradual progress in your fitness routine is crucial to avoid burnout and ensure long-term success. Here's how to do it:

1. Start Slow and Steady:

Begin your fitness journey with a manageable pace. Avoid the temptation to jump into intense workouts right away. Gradual progression allows your body and mind to adapt, reducing the risk of physical and mental burnout.

2. Set Achievable Goals:

Establish goals that are realistic and attainable. Break down larger objectives into smaller milestones, celebrating each achievement along the way. Achieving these goals provides a sense of accomplishment and motivates you to continue.

3. Embrace Incremental Changes:

Gradual progress involves making small, incremental changes to your routine. Whether it's increasing workout duration by five minutes each week or adding a bit more weight to your strength training, these subtle adjustments can lead to significant improvements over time.

4. Listen to Your Body:

Pay close attention to your body's signals. If you experience persistent fatigue, soreness, or discomfort, it's a sign that you may be pushing too hard. Give yourself permission to rest and recover when needed.

5. Incorporate Rest and Recovery:

Rest days are essential for avoiding burnout. They allow your muscles to repair, and your mind to recharge. Schedule regular rest days into your workout routine to prevent physical and mental exhaustion.

6. Vary Intensity:

Avoid consistently high-intensity workouts. Incorporate periods of lower-intensity activities, such as gentle yoga or leisurely walks, to provide your body and mind with a break while still staying active.

7. Cross-Train:

Cross-training involves alternating between different types of exercise. It not only reduces the risk of overuse injuries but also keeps your workouts engaging and diverse, preventing mental monotony.

8. Use Periodization:

Periodization is a training technique that involves cycling between periods of different intensities and focuses. It helps prevent plateaus and keeps your workouts stimulating. For example, you might have phases of strength training, followed by a period of endurance training.

9. Prioritize Recovery Techniques:

Incorporate recovery techniques like stretching, foam rolling, and mindfulness practices into your routine. These activities promote relaxation, reduce stress, and aid in physical recovery.

10. Set Realistic Expectations:

Accept that progress may be slower than you initially anticipated. Be patient with yourself and recognize that steady, sustainable progress is more important than rapid results.

11. Seek Professional Guidance:

Consider consulting with a fitness professional or trainer who can design a progressive and balanced workout plan tailored to your needs and goals.

12. Keep It Enjoyable:

Above all, ensure that your fitness routine remains enjoyable. If you dread your workouts, it's more likely that burnout will occur. Choose activities you genuinely love, and find joy in the journey.

Sample Progression:

Here's an example of how you can gradually progress in your fitness routine:

- ◇ Week 1: Start with 20 minutes of brisk walking three days a week.

- ◇ Week 2: Increase walking duration to 25 minutes, maintaining the same frequency.

- ◇ Week 3: Add one day of strength training with light weights (20 minutes).

◇ Week 4: Extend strength training to two days a week, still with light weights.

◇ Week 5: Increase walking duration to 30 minutes and continue strength training.

Building for Long-Term Success

Building gradual progress and avoiding burnout are fundamental to establishing a sustainable fitness routine that supports your mental health. Remember that your fitness journey is a marathon, not a sprint. By taking incremental steps, listening to your body, and making adjustments as needed, you can create a routine that serves your well-being in the long run.

Incorporating Mindfulness into Your Workouts

Imagine a calm and tranquil river flowing alongside a well-trodden path. This river represents mindfulness, and by incorporating it into your workouts, you can infuse your fitness routine with a deep sense of presence and well-being. Here's how to embrace mindfulness during your physical activity:

1. Mindful Warm-Up:

Begin your workout with a mindful warm-up. Rather than rushing through stretching and mobility exercises, focus on each movement. Pay attention to the sensations in your body, your breath, and the way your muscles respond to the stretches.

2. Concentrate on Breath:

Throughout your workout, maintain awareness of your breath. Notice the rhythm of your inhalations and exhalations. Breathing mindfully can help you stay centered and calm, even during challenging exercises.

3. Engage Your Senses:

Use your senses to anchor yourself in the present moment. Observe the sights, sounds, and sensations around you. Whether you're in a gym, a park, or your own home, let your surroundings become part of your mindful experience.

4. Body Scan:

Periodically conduct a body scan. Start at your toes and work your way up to your head, paying attention to any areas of tension or discomfort. Mindful awareness can help you identify and release physical and mental stress.

5. Intention Setting:

Before each workout, set an intention. This could be related to your mental health goals, such as reducing stress or finding inner peace. Remind yourself of your intention as you move through your workout.

6. Mindful Movement:

Perform exercises with intention and awareness. Whether you're lifting weights, running, or doing yoga, focus on the quality of your movements. Notice how your body feels during each repetition or pose.

7. Embrace Mindful Cardio:

During aerobic exercises like running, cycling, or swimming, let your mind flow with the rhythm of your activity. Pay attention to the sensation of your heart beating and the steady flow of breath.

8. Guided Meditation:

Consider incorporating short guided meditations into your workout. These can be as simple as a five-minute breathing exercise or a guided visualization session. There are many apps and online resources available for this purpose.

9. Cool-Down Reflection:

As you conclude your workout, take a few moments for reflection. Consider what you've accomplished physically and mentally during your session. Acknowledge any stress you've released or positive emotions you've cultivated.

10. Mindful Hydration and Nutrition:

Extend mindfulness beyond your workout. Pay attention to your hydration and nutrition, which play a crucial role in mental health. Mindfully nourish your body to support your overall well-being.

11. Gratitude Practice:

Express gratitude for your ability to engage in physical activity. Whether it's a simple "thank you" to your body or a mental acknowledgment of the opportunity to move, gratitude can enhance your workout experience.

12. Savasana or Cool-Down Meditation:

If you're doing yoga or another mind-body practice, finish with a mindful savasana or cool-down meditation. Allow yourself to fully relax and absorb the mental benefits of your practice.

The Mindful Workout Experience

Incorporating mindfulness into your workouts transforms exercise into a holistic practice for mental and physical well-being. As you embrace the present moment, your fitness routine becomes not only a path to improved physical health but also a journey toward inner peace, stress reduction, and enhanced mental resilience.

The Role of Accountability Partners and Support Systems

Imagine embarking on a challenging hike through a dense forest. Having a trusted companion by your side can make the journey more manageable and enjoyable. Similarly, accountability partners and support systems play a crucial role in your fitness journey. Here's how they can enhance your mental health through physical activity:

1. Motivation and Encouragement:

Accountability partners provide motivation and encouragement when you need it most. Knowing that someone is counting on you to show up for a workout can be a powerful incentive to stay committed, even on tough days.

2. Shared Goals and Progress:

When you have a support system, you can share your fitness goals and track your progress together. This creates a sense of camaraderie and shared achievement, boosting your confidence and sense of accomplishment.

3. Consistency:

Accountability partners help maintain consistency in your workout routine. Knowing that you have regular workout dates or check-ins with someone can prevent you from skipping sessions.

4. Increased Commitment:

When you commit to someone else, you're more likely to follow through. Accountability partners hold you responsible for your fitness goals, reinforcing your dedication to mental well-being.

5. Feedback and Guidance:

Support systems can provide valuable feedback and guidance. Whether it's advice on exercise techniques, workout plans, or nutrition, the insights of others can enhance your fitness journey.

6. Emotional Support:

Physical activity can be emotionally challenging, especially when dealing with stress, anxiety, or depression. Having someone to lean on during these times can make a significant difference in your mental health journey.

7. Social Interaction:

Engaging in physical activity with others offers social interaction, which is essential for mental well-being. Whether it's participating in group fitness classes, joining a sports team, or walking with a friend, these connections foster a sense of community.

8. Accountability Apps and Platforms:

In addition to human accountability partners, various apps and online platforms can help you stay on track. These tools allow you to set goals, track progress, and connect with a community of like-minded individuals.

9. Celebrating Achievements:

Accountability partners and support systems celebrate your achievements, no matter how small. Recognizing your successes reinforces positive behaviors and boosts your self-esteem.

10. Creating Healthy Habits:

Having someone to be accountable to helps you establish healthy habits beyond your workouts. These habits, such as proper nutrition and adequate sleep, contribute significantly to mental health.

11. Building Resilience:

The support of others can help you build mental resilience. When facing setbacks or challenges, your accountability partners can offer a helping hand and remind you of your progress.

12. Expanding Your Network:

Engaging in fitness activities with others can expand your social network. Meeting new people who share your interests can lead to lasting friendships and a stronger support system.

Choosing the Right Partners

When selecting accountability partners and support systems, consider individuals who align with your goals and values. Whether it's a friend, family member, fitness buddy, or an online community, the right partners can make a significant impact on your mental health journey through physical activity.

Chapter 8: Mindful Movement: Yoga and Meditation

Exploring the Mental Health Benefits of Yoga

Imagine yourself in a serene, sunlit room, surrounded by tranquility. This setting embodies the essence of yoga, a practice that extends beyond physical flexibility and strength. Yoga is a holistic approach to wellness that significantly contributes to mental health. Here are some of the key mental health benefits of yoga:

1. Stress Reduction:

Yoga emphasizes relaxation and mindfulness, both of which are effective in reducing stress. Through controlled breathing (pranayama) and meditative techniques, yoga helps calm the nervous system, lowering cortisol levels and promoting a sense of inner peace.

2. Anxiety Management:

Yoga offers valuable tools for managing anxiety. The practice encourages present-moment awareness, allowing individuals to observe anxious thoughts without judgment. Over time, this can lead to reduced anxiety and increased emotional resilience.

3. Alleviation of Depression Symptoms:

Yoga has been shown to alleviate symptoms of depression. Regular practice can enhance mood and increase the production of feel-good neurotransmitters like serotonin. It also provides a sense of purpose and accomplishment, which can combat the lethargy often associated with depression.

4. Improved Emotional Regulation:

Yoga enhances emotional regulation by teaching practitioners to respond to emotions rather than react impulsively. This can lead to greater emotional stability and a more positive outlook on life.

5. Enhanced Mindfulness:

Mindfulness is at the core of yoga practice. By focusing on breath and body sensations, yoga cultivates mindfulness skills that can be applied to daily life. This heightened awareness helps individuals better manage emotions and stressors.

6. Better Sleep Quality:

Yoga can improve sleep quality, which is essential for mental health. Mindful relaxation techniques and specific postures can promote restful sleep and alleviate insomnia.

7. Increased Self-Esteem:

As individuals progress in their yoga practice, they often experience a sense of accomplishment and empowerment. This increased self-esteem can have a positive ripple effect on overall mental well-being.

8. Body-Mind Connection:

Yoga fosters a strong connection between the body and mind. This awareness allows individuals to better understand and address the physical and emotional sensations they experience.

9. Social Connection:

Participating in group yoga classes or joining a yoga community provides a sense of social connection, reducing feelings of isolation and loneliness that can negatively impact mental health.

10. Coping with Trauma:

Yoga can be a valuable tool for individuals coping with trauma. Mindful movement and breathing can help process difficult emotions and promote healing.

11. Building Resilience:

Regular yoga practice can build mental resilience by teaching individuals to face challenges with equanimity and adaptability. This resilience can be applied to various aspects of life.

12. Cultivating Gratitude:

Yoga encourages a sense of gratitude for the body and its capabilities. This appreciation can lead to a more positive attitude and improved mental well-being.

Sample Yoga Practice:

Here's a simple yoga practice that can promote mental health:

◇ Begin with deep, mindful breathing for a few minutes to center yourself.

◇ Practice a series of gentle stretches and postures, focusing on your breath and bodily sensations.

◇ Incorporate meditation or mindfulness exercises into your practice, such as body scanning or loving-kindness meditation.

◇ Finish with a few minutes of Savasana (corpse pose) for deep relaxation.

Holistic Well-Being through Yoga

Yoga is a holistic practice that addresses the interconnectedness of the body and mind. By exploring the mental health benefits of yoga, individuals can enhance their emotional resilience, reduce stress, and develop a profound sense of well-being. Incorporating yoga into your routine can be a transformative step toward improved mental health.

Incorporating Mindfulness into Your Practice

Imagine yourself on a yoga mat, each movement and breath synchronized with a profound sense of presence. This is the essence of mindfulness in yoga—a practice that enriches both body and mind. Here's how to seamlessly incorporate mindfulness into your yoga practice for maximum mental health benefits:

1. Begin with Intention:

Before you step onto your yoga mat, set a clear intention for your practice. This could be related to your mental health goals, such as reducing stress or increasing self-compassion. Visualize how you want to feel both physically and mentally at the end of your session.

2. Focus on Your Breath:

Throughout your practice, anchor your attention to your breath. Notice the rhythm of your inhalations and exhalations. The breath serves as a constant reminder to stay present and centered.

3. Body Awareness:

As you move through different yoga poses, cultivate body awareness. Pay attention to the sensations in your muscles, joints, and the physical alignment of your body. This heightened awareness deepens your connection to the present moment.

4. Mindful Transitions:

Mindfulness extends to the transitions between poses. Rather than rushing from one posture to the next, move deliberately and with full awareness. Each transition is an opportunity to practice mindfulness.

5. Use Mantras or Affirmations:

Incorporate mantras or affirmations that resonate with your mental health goals. Repeat them silently or audibly during your practice to reinforce positive intentions.

6. Savor Stillness:

Yoga includes moments of stillness, such as in Savasana (corpse pose) or meditation. Embrace these moments fully. Let go of distractions and immerse yourself in the calm and quiet, allowing your mind to settle.

7. Mindful Meditation:

Integrate mindfulness meditation into your practice. This can involve focused breathing, body scans, or loving-kindness meditation. These practices enhance emotional regulation and cultivate inner peace.

8. Non-Judgmental Observation:

Practice non-judgmental observation of your thoughts and emotions. When distracting thoughts arise, acknowledge them without criticism and gently return your focus to your breath or the present moment.

9. Gratitude and Self-Compassion:

During your practice, express gratitude for your body and its capabilities. Extend self-compassion to yourself, recognizing that you are doing your best in this moment.

10. Savasana as Mindfulness:

Use Savasana as an opportunity to deepen your mindfulness practice. Let go of tension in every part of your body and release any mental stress. This final relaxation is a time to integrate the physical and mental benefits of your practice.

11. Reflect and Journal:

After your yoga practice, take a few moments to reflect on your experience. Consider how the mindfulness techniques influenced your mental state. You can also maintain a yoga journal to track your progress and insights.

12. Carry Mindfulness Beyond the Mat:

Extend mindfulness beyond your yoga mat. Apply the principles of mindfulness, such as present-moment awareness and non-judgmental observation, to your daily life. This integration can have a profound and lasting impact on your mental health.

Sample Mindful Yoga Practice:

Here's a brief outline of a mindful yoga practice:

> ◈ Begin in a comfortable seated position, setting your intention for the practice.

> ◈ Focus on your breath, taking a few deep inhales and exhales.

> ◈ Flow through a series of yoga poses with mindful transitions.

> ◈ Incorporate meditation or mantra repetition during poses or in between.

> ◈ Spend several minutes in Savasana, fully embracing stillness and mindfulness.

> ◈ Conclude with gratitude and a brief reflection on your practice.

The Mindful Yoga Experience

Incorporating mindfulness into your yoga practice elevates it beyond physical exercise. It becomes a transformative journey that nurtures both your body and mind. By weaving mindfulness into your yoga routine, you can unlock the full potential of yoga's mental health benefits and experience profound well-being.

Guided Meditation and Its Impact on Well-Being

Imagine a tranquil garden, where a gentle guide leads you along a serene path. This is the essence of guided meditation—a practice that can significantly enhance your mental well-being. Here's how guided meditation can positively impact your overall well-being when integrated into your physical activity routine:

1. Stress Reduction:

Guided meditation is a potent stress-reduction technique. By following a soothing voice, you can relax both your body and mind, allowing stress and tension to melt away. Regular practice leads to reduced cortisol levels and a calmer nervous system.

2. Anxiety Management:

Guided meditation provides valuable tools for managing anxiety. The guided sessions often include techniques for grounding, deep breathing, and calming visualization. These practices help individuals become more resilient to anxious thoughts and emotions.

3. Enhanced Mindfulness:

Guided meditation strengthens mindfulness skills. It encourages you to focus your attention on the present moment, cultivating self-awareness and promoting emotional regulation.

4. Improved Concentration:

Meditation enhances concentration and mental clarity. As you practice guided meditation, you train your mind to remain attentive and focused, which can benefit various aspects of your life.

5. Emotional Resilience:

Guided meditation builds emotional resilience by teaching individuals to respond to emotions with equanimity. This can help individuals better cope with life's challenges and maintain a positive outlook.

6. Better Sleep Quality:

Guided meditation can alleviate insomnia and improve sleep quality. The practice promotes relaxation and reduces the racing thoughts that often interfere with restful sleep.

7. Self-Compassion:

Guided meditations often include self-compassion exercises. By practicing self-kindness and self-acceptance, individuals can boost their self-esteem and overall well-being.

8. Empowerment:

Guided meditation fosters a sense of empowerment. It encourages individuals to take charge of their mental health and well-being by providing them with tools to manage their inner world.

9. Emotional Release:

During guided meditation, individuals may experience emotional release. This process allows for the safe expression and processing of pent-up emotions, contributing to mental and emotional healing.

10. Mind-Body Connection:

Guided meditation strengthens the mind-body connection. It helps individuals recognize and address physical sensations associated with emotions, promoting holistic well-being.

11. Gratitude and Positivity:

Many guided meditations focus on gratitude and positive affirmations. These practices cultivate a positive mindset, enhancing overall mental health.

12. Coping with Trauma:

Guided meditation can be a valuable tool for individuals coping with trauma. It provides a safe space to explore difficult emotions and promote healing.

Sample Guided Meditation Practice:

Here's a simple outline for a guided meditation practice:

1. Find a quiet and comfortable space to sit or lie down.

2. Begin with deep, mindful breaths to center yourself.

3. Play a guided meditation recording or use a meditation app.

4. Follow the voice of the guide as they lead you through relaxation and mindfulness exercises.

5. Allow yourself to fully immerse in the experience, letting go of distractions.

6. Conclude the session with a few moments of silent reflection.

7. Gradually return to your surroundings, feeling refreshed and grounded.

A Journey to Inner Peace

Guided meditation is a journey to inner peace and well-being. By integrating this practice into your fitness routine, you can harness its transformative power and experience a profound sense of mental calm and resilience. Guided meditation becomes a valuable companion on your path to improved mental health.

Testimonials from Individuals Who Found Peace Through Yoga

Testimonial 1: Sarah's Journey to Inner Calm

Sarah, a 34-year-old marketing executive, had always been a go-getter. Her busy life left little room for self-care, and stress began to take its toll. "I was constantly on the edge," she recalls. "Anxiety and restlessness were my constant companions."

Desperate for relief, Sarah decided to give yoga a try. "My first class was a revelation," she says. "The soothing environment, gentle movements, and focus on breath made me feel like I had found an oasis of calm in the midst of chaos."

As Sarah continued her yoga practice, she noticed a significant shift in her mental state. "Yoga taught me to let go of my racing thoughts and be present," she shares. "The more I practiced, the less anxious I became. I found a sense of inner peace I never thought possible."

Testimonial 2: Mark's Battle with Depression

Mark, a 42-year-old teacher, had been battling depression for years. He tried various therapies and medications, but the cloud of darkness never truly lifted. "I felt like I was stuck in a never-ending storm," he says.

One day, a friend suggested he join a yoga class. Mark was skeptical but decided to give it a shot. "From the very first session, I felt a glimmer of hope," he remembers. "Yoga gave me a sense of purpose and a reason to get out of bed."

Through consistent yoga practice, Mark began to experience subtle but profound changes. "Yoga made me more attuned to my body and emotions," he explains. "It allowed me to observe my thoughts without judgment. Over time, I felt a lightness I hadn't felt in years."

Testimonial 3: Grace's Recovery from Trauma

Grace, a 29-year-old trauma survivor, had spent years trying to suppress painful memories and emotions. "I felt like I was carrying a heavy burden," she says. "I couldn't move forward because the past was holding me back."

On the advice of her therapist, Grace started practicing trauma-informed yoga. "Yoga gave me a safe space to explore my body and release trapped emotions," she shares. "The practice allowed me to regain a sense of control and reconnect with my body in a positive way."

Over time, Grace found peace through yoga. "I learned to treat myself with kindness and compassion," she says. "Yoga became my refuge—a place where I could heal and rebuild my life."

Testimonial 4: David's Journey to Self-Discovery

David, a 50-year-old retiree, had always put others' needs before his own. He found himself yearning for a deeper sense of purpose and self-discovery in his post-retirement life.

Discovering yoga was a turning point for David. "Yoga gave me the opportunity to explore my inner world," he explains. "Through the practice, I began to unravel layers of myself I had long ignored."

David's yoga journey led to profound self-discovery and a newfound sense of peace. "I realized that taking care of my mental and emotional well-being was just as important as my physical health," he reflects. "Yoga became a lifelong journey of self-love and personal growth."

Testimonial 5: Sophia's Journey to Mindful Living

Sophia, a 38-year-old mother of two, was constantly juggling family and work responsibilities. She often felt overwhelmed and disconnected from herself. "I felt like I was losing touch with who I was," she admits.

Yoga became a lifeline for Sophia. "It was a gift to myself," she says. "Yoga allowed me to slow down, breathe, and rediscover my inner strength."

Through her yoga practice, Sophia found a sense of balance and mindfulness in her daily life. "I learned that self-care isn't selfish; it's essential," she emphasizes. "Yoga helped me become a more present and compassionate mother, partner, and person."

Testimonials That Inspire

These testimonials from individuals who found peace through yoga demonstrate the profound impact of this practice on mental health and well-being. Each story reflects a unique journey of self-discovery, healing, and inner peace.

Chapter 9: The Healing Power of Nature

Nature's Impact on Mental Health

Imagine standing at the edge of a tranquil forest, the scent of pine in the air, and the gentle rustling of leaves in the wind. Nature has a unique way of soothing the soul and nurturing mental well-being. Here's how nature's impact on mental health can be transformative:

1. Stress Reduction:

Nature provides a serene escape from the demands and stressors of daily life. Spending time in natural settings, such as forests, parks, or near bodies of water, has been shown to reduce cortisol levels, the stress hormone.

2. Mood Enhancement:

Interacting with nature triggers the release of endorphins, the body's natural mood lifters. The sights, sounds, and smells of nature can instantly boost your spirits and reduce feelings of sadness or anxiety.

3. Improved Concentration:

Nature offers a restorative environment for the brain. Time spent in natural settings has been linked to improved focus and concentration, making it an excellent antidote to mental fatigue.

4. Enhanced Creativity:

Nature fosters creativity by providing a break from the mental clutter of everyday life. The beauty and unpredictability of the natural world can inspire fresh ideas and innovative thinking.

5. Mindfulness and Present-Moment Awareness:

Nature naturally encourages mindfulness—the practice of being fully present in the moment. When immersed in nature, you're more likely to notice the intricate details, colors, and textures around you, which promotes a sense of grounding and awareness.

6. Emotional Resilience:

Regular exposure to nature has been linked to increased emotional resilience. The ability to bounce back from stress and adversity is a key component of mental well-being.

7. Social Connection:

Engaging in outdoor activities with friends or family enhances social bonds, which are essential for mental health. Nature provides a backdrop for shared experiences and meaningful connections.

8. Time for Reflection:

Natural settings offer a peaceful space for reflection and introspection. Whether you're hiking in the mountains or sitting by a quiet pond, nature encourages self-discovery and a deeper understanding of your own thoughts and feelings.

9. Physical Activity and Nature:

Combining physical activity with time in nature amplifies the mental health benefits. Activities like hiking, biking, or simply walking in a natural environment provide a double dose of well-being.

10. Stress Resilience:

Spending time in nature can improve your ability to cope with stress. Exposure to natural surroundings can make you more adaptable and less prone to the negative effects of chronic stress.

11. Increased Sense of Awe:

Nature often evokes feelings of awe and wonder. Experiencing the vastness and beauty of the natural world can shift your perspective and remind you of the interconnectedness of all life.

12. A Sense of Belonging:

Connecting with nature can instill a sense of belonging to a larger ecosystem. This feeling of interconnectedness can provide a deeper sense of purpose and meaning in life.

Sample Nature-Based Activities:

◈ Go for a leisurely hike in a nearby nature reserve.

◈ Take a calming stroll along a beach or lakefront.

◈ Practice mindfulness in a forest, paying attention to the sights and sounds around you.

◈ Engage in birdwatching or wildlife observation.

◈ Try forest bathing, a Japanese practice of immersing yourself in the forest atmosphere.

The Natural Path to Well-Being

Nature's impact on mental health is profound and well-documented. By intentionally incorporating time in natural settings into your routine, you can harness its therapeutic power to reduce stress, enhance mood, and foster a sense of well-being. Nature becomes a trusted ally on your journey toward improved mental health.

Outdoor Activities and Their Therapeutic Benefits

Imagine yourself on a sun-dappled trail, surrounded by the vibrant colors of nature. Each step you take feels like a step toward inner peace and mental well-being. Outdoor activities in natural settings provide unique therapeutic benefits:

1. Hiking and Nature Walks:

Hiking through forests, along mountainsides, or beside serene lakes offers not only physical exercise but also the chance to connect with the natural world. The rhythmic movement, fresh air, and captivating scenery promote relaxation and mindfulness.

2. Gardening:

Tending to a garden, whether it's a small plot or a few potted plants, can be a therapeutic and grounding experience. Gardening encourages mindfulness, as you focus on nurturing and watching life bloom and thrive.

3. Camping:

Camping allows you to disconnect from the hustle and bustle of daily life and immerse yourself in nature. The simplicity of outdoor living can reduce stress and foster a sense of self-sufficiency.

4. Water-Based Activities:

Activities like kayaking, paddleboarding, or even a leisurely swim provide a unique connection with natural bodies of water. Water-based activities are known for their calming and soothing effects on the mind.

5. Birdwatching and Wildlife Observation:

Observing birds and wildlife in their natural habitat can be a meditative practice. It encourages present-moment awareness and an appreciation for the beauty of the natural world.

6. Cycling:

Cycling combines physical activity with the joy of exploring outdoor landscapes. Whether it's a leisurely ride through the countryside or a more intense mountain biking adventure, cycling provides a sense of freedom and exhilaration.

7. Rock Climbing and Bouldering:

Scaling cliffs and boulders challenges both body and mind. These activities promote focus, problem-solving, and a sense of accomplishment as you conquer new heights.

8. Forest Bathing (Shinrin-Yoku):

Forest bathing, a Japanese practice, involves immersing yourself in a forest environment. It encourages mindful walking and meditation in nature, promoting relaxation and stress reduction.

9. Picnicking and Outdoor Dining:

Eating in natural settings, such as a park or near a river, can turn a meal into a sensory experience. It's an opportunity to savor flavors, enjoy the company of others, and connect with nature.

10. Stargazing:

Spending time under the night sky, observing stars and celestial bodies, can instill a sense of wonder and perspective. Stargazing encourages reflection and contemplation.

11. Trail Running:

Trail running combines the physical benefits of running with the mental benefits of being in nature. The uneven terrain and changing scenery keep your mind engaged and present.

12. Nature Art and Photography:

Engaging in creative pursuits in natural settings, such as sketching, painting, or photography, can be a therapeutic outlet for self-expression and mindfulness.

Sample Outdoor Activity: Forest Bathing

Here's a brief outline for a forest bathing session:

1. Find a quiet forest or natural area.

2. Disconnect from electronic devices.

3. Walk slowly and mindfully, paying attention to your surroundings.

4. Engage your senses by observing the sights, sounds, and scents of the forest.

5. Pause to meditate or sit quietly and listen to the sounds of nature.

6. Reflect on your experience and express gratitude for the natural world.

Embracing the Healing Outdoors

Outdoor activities provide a myriad of therapeutic benefits for mental well-being. Whether you're seeking relaxation, adventure, or simply a moment of mindfulness, the great outdoors offers a welcoming space for rejuvenation and healing. By incorporating outdoor activities into your routine, you can tap into nature's inherent capacity to nurture and restore your mental health.

Mindful Hiking, Forest Bathing, and Ecotherapy

Imagine yourself on a quiet forest trail, with each step carrying you deeper into the embrace of nature. As you move through the wilderness, you're not just hiking; you're practicing mindfulness, engaging in forest bathing, and participating in ecotherapy. These practices enrich your connection with the natural world and provide unique mental health benefits:

1. Mindful Hiking:

Mindful hiking is a practice that combines the physical activity of hiking with the mindfulness of meditation. It encourages you to be fully present in the natural environment, engaging all your senses as you move through it. Here's how it can benefit your mental well-being:

◇ **Presence and Awareness:** Mindful hiking cultivates presence and awareness. You learn to notice the details of the trail—the feel of the earth beneath your feet, the rustling of leaves, and the scent of the forest.

◈ **Stress Reduction:** By immersing yourself in the sights and sounds of nature, mindful hiking reduces stress and anxiety. It's an opportunity to leave behind the worries of daily life and find solace in the natural world.

◈ **Improved Focus:** As you practice mindfulness during hiking, your ability to focus and concentrate can improve. This heightened focus can carry over to other areas of your life.

2. Forest Bathing (Shinrin-Yoku):

Forest bathing, or Shinrin-Yoku, is a Japanese practice that involves immersing yourself in a forest environment. It's a form of nature therapy that promotes relaxation and well-being. Here's how it contributes to mental health:

◈ **Stress Reduction:** Spending time in the forest environment reduces cortisol levels, the stress hormone. The sights, sounds, and scents of the forest induce a deep sense of calm and tranquility.

◈ **Mindful Connection:** Forest bathing encourages mindful walking and meditation in nature. It provides an opportunity to disconnect from electronic devices and engage with the natural world.

◈ **Enhanced Mood:** Time in the forest has been associated with improved mood and a reduction in symptoms of depression and anxiety. The beauty and serenity of nature lift the spirits.

3. Ecotherapy:

Ecotherapy, or nature-based therapy, is a therapeutic approach that integrates outdoor activities and natural settings into the healing process. It recognizes the profound impact of nature on mental well-being. Here's how ecotherapy can benefit individuals:

◈ **Emotional Healing:** Ecotherapy allows individuals to explore their emotions and experiences in a natural setting. This can lead to emotional healing and growth.

◈ **Strengthened Resilience:** Engaging in ecotherapy can build emotional resilience, helping individuals better cope with life's challenges and stressors.

◈ **Self-Reflection:** Nature provides a tranquil backdrop for self-reflection and introspection. It's a space to gain insights into one's thoughts, feelings, and life path.

Sample Mindful Hiking Practice:

Here's a simple outline for a mindful hiking practice:

1. Choose a hiking trail that aligns with your fitness level and time constraints.

2. Begin the hike with a few moments of deep breathing to center yourself.

3. As you hike, engage your senses—notice the textures, colors, and sounds around you.

4. Stay present by continually bringing your focus back to the natural environment whenever your mind wanders.

5. Pause at various points along the trail to meditate or simply be still and observe.

6. Complete the hike with gratitude for the rejuvenating experience.

The Healing Embrace of Nature

Mindful hiking, forest bathing, and ecotherapy are profound ways to harness the healing power of nature for mental well-being. They offer an opportunity to disconnect from the busyness of modern life and reconnect with the natural world and, in turn, with yourself. By incorporating these practices into your routine, you can experience the transformative benefits of nature on your mental health.

Personal Stories of Nature's Transformative Power

Story 1: Emma's Journey to Recovery

Emma, a 28-year-old artist, had been struggling with anxiety and depression for years. The weight of her emotions often left her feeling overwhelmed and disconnected from herself. It wasn't until she decided to take a solo backpacking trip through the Appalachian Trail that she found solace.

"For the first time, I felt truly alive," Emma recalls. "Surrounded by the grandeur of the mountains and the tranquility of the forest, I could breathe freely. Nature embraced me without judgment."

Emma's journey through the wilderness became a mirror for her inner journey to recovery. The solitude allowed her to confront her deepest fears and anxieties. "I realized that nature was my greatest therapist," she says. "It offered me the space to heal and find strength within myself."

Story 2: Samuel's Escape to Serenity

Samuel, a 45-year-old corporate executive, had been caught in the relentless grind of city life. The constant demands of his career left him burnt out and emotionally drained. One day, a close friend invited him on a kayaking trip down a quiet river.

"As I paddled down that river, something inside me shifted," Samuel recounts. "The gentle rhythm of the water, the rustling leaves, and the chirping birds created a symphony of peace I had long forgotten."

That kayaking trip became a turning point for Samuel. He began spending weekends in natural settings, embracing activities like camping and hiking. "Nature became my sanctuary," he says. "It offered me a refuge from the chaos of urban life and allowed me to rediscover my inner calm."

Story 3: Maria's Path to Healing

Maria, a 38-year-old therapist, had dedicated her life to helping others overcome their mental health challenges. But she often neglected her own well-being. After a particularly demanding year at work, she decided to embark on a pilgrimage along the Camino de Santiago in Spain.

"The Camino was a journey of self-discovery," Maria shares. "Walking day after day through picturesque landscapes, I had time to confront my own unresolved issues and find healing."

Maria's connection to nature, as she walked through forests, fields, and mountains, mirrored her inner journey toward emotional healing. "Nature mirrored the cycles of life, death, and rebirth," she reflects. "It reminded me that healing is an ongoing process, and I needed to extend the same compassion to myself that I offered my clients."

Story 4: Thomas's Connection with the Elements

Thomas, a 53-year-old retired teacher, had always felt a deep affinity for the natural world. He had spent his childhood exploring the woods and fields near his home, but as an adult, the demands of life had pulled him away from his beloved nature.

Upon retirement, Thomas decided to rekindle his connection with the elements. He began practicing mindfulness meditation by a serene lake and took up photography as a way to capture the beauty he found in nature.

"Reconnecting with nature brought me a profound sense of contentment," Thomas reflects. "The simple act of sitting by the lake, feeling the breeze, and listening to the gentle lapping of the water was my daily therapy."

Story 5: Lily's Healing Garden

Lily, a 62-year-old retiree, had always been an avid gardener. When she faced a period of grief and loss after the passing of her spouse, her garden became her sanctuary.

"Working in the garden was a form of meditation for me," Lily shares. "As I planted, nurtured, and watched life bloom, I found solace and hope."

Lily's healing journey was deeply intertwined with her garden. She found that the act of tending to living things allowed her to process her grief and find moments of peace and joy.

Stories That Inspire Connection

These personal stories of nature's transformative power demonstrate the profound impact of the natural world on mental well-being. Nature, in its beauty and simplicity, offers a path to healing, self-discovery, and emotional growth. May these stories inspire your own connection with nature and its potential to transform your mental health.

Chapter 10: Nutrition and Mental Wellness

The Link Between Diet and Mental Health

Imagine your body as a finely tuned instrument, with each nutrient representing a note in a harmonious melody. Your diet forms the foundation of this composition, influencing the state of your mental health in profound ways. Here's how the link between diet and mental health can be transformative:

1. Nutrient Deficiencies and Mood:

Your brain requires a balanced intake of essential nutrients to function optimally. Nutrient deficiencies can lead to mood disturbances, cognitive decline, and an increased risk of mental health disorders.

2. Gut-Brain Connection:

The gut and brain are intricately connected through the gut-brain axis. A healthy gut microbiome is essential for mental well-being. Diet can either nurture or disrupt this delicate balance, influencing your mood and emotional resilience.

3. Inflammation and Mental Health:

Chronic inflammation in the body has been linked to various mental health conditions, including depression and anxiety. Certain foods can either promote or reduce inflammation, affecting your emotional state.

4. Blood Sugar Regulation:

Balancing blood sugar levels through a mindful diet can prevent mood swings and irritability. Stable blood sugar levels support consistent energy and emotional stability.

5. Neurotransmitters and Diet:

Neurotransmitters like serotonin and dopamine, which regulate mood, are influenced by the availability of specific nutrients. Your diet can impact the production and function of these vital chemicals.

6. Antioxidants and Brain Health:

Antioxidants found in fruits, vegetables, and whole grains protect the brain from oxidative stress. A diet rich in antioxidants supports cognitive function and emotional well-being.

7. Omega-3 Fatty Acids:

Omega-3 fatty acids, primarily found in fatty fish, walnuts, and flaxseeds, are essential for brain health. They have been linked to reduced symptoms of depression and anxiety.

8. Hydration and Cognitive Function:

Dehydration can impair cognitive function and mood. Staying adequately hydrated is crucial for maintaining mental clarity and emotional stability.

9. Mindful Eating and Emotional Awareness:

Practicing mindful eating, where you pay attention to the colors, textures, and flavors of your food, can enhance your emotional awareness. It helps you recognize the connection between your diet and your mood.

10. Dietary Patterns and Mental Health:

Certain dietary patterns, such as the Mediterranean diet and the DASH diet (Dietary Approaches to Stop Hypertension), have been associated with a lower risk of mental health disorders. These diets prioritize whole foods, fruits, vegetables, and lean proteins.

Sample Mood-Boosting Foods:

◇ **Berries:** Rich in antioxidants that support brain health.

◇ **Leafy Greens:** High in folate, a nutrient linked to mood regulation.

◇ **Fatty Fish (e.g., salmon, mackerel):** Source of omega-3 fatty acids.

◇ **Nuts and Seeds:** Provide essential nutrients for brain health.

◇ **Whole Grains:** Support stable blood sugar levels.

◇ **Probiotic Foods (e.g., yogurt, kefir):** Promote a healthy gut microbiome.

◇ **Dark Chocolate (in moderation):** Contains mood-enhancing compounds.

The Nutritional Symphony of Mental Wellness

Your diet is the symphony conductor of your mental wellness, influencing the melody of your emotions and cognitive function. By nourishing your body with a mindful and balanced diet, you can compose a harmonious tune of mental health.

Nutritional Strategies to Support Mental Well-Being

Picture your body as a canvas, and the foods you consume as the vibrant colors that paint your mental landscape. The right nutritional strategies can help you create a masterpiece of mental well-being:

1. Balanced Diet:

A balanced diet provides your brain with the essential nutrients it needs. Ensure your meals include a variety of whole foods, including fruits, vegetables, lean proteins, whole grains, and healthy fats. Avoid excessive consumption of processed foods and sugary beverages.

2. Omega-3 Fatty Acids:

Incorporate omega-3-rich foods into your diet. Fatty fish like salmon, mackerel, and sardines, as well as plant sources like flaxseeds and walnuts, contain these essential fatty acids. Omega-3s have been associated with improved mood and reduced symptoms of depression.

3. Complex Carbohydrates:

Choose complex carbohydrates over refined sugars. Whole grains, legumes, and vegetables release glucose slowly, providing a steady supply of energy to the brain and stabilizing your mood.

4. Antioxidant-Rich Foods:

Foods rich in antioxidants, such as berries, dark leafy greens, and colorful fruits, help protect your brain from oxidative stress. These compounds promote cognitive function and emotional well-being.

5. Probiotic Foods:

A healthy gut microbiome is crucial for mental health. Incorporate probiotic-rich foods like yogurt, kefir, sauerkraut, and kimchi into your diet to support gut health and a balanced mood.

6. Hydration:

Stay adequately hydrated throughout the day. Dehydration can impair cognitive function and mood. Aim to drink plenty of water and limit the consumption of sugary or caffeinated beverages.

7. Mindful Eating:

Practice mindful eating by savoring each bite, paying attention to the colors and textures of your food, and chewing slowly. This approach enhances your connection to the sensory experience of eating and can improve your emotional awareness.

8. Limit Processed Foods:

Processed foods often contain high levels of added sugars, unhealthy fats, and artificial additives. These ingredients can negatively impact mood and cognitive function. Minimize your intake of processed and fast foods.

9. Moderation with Caffeine and Alcohol:

While caffeine and alcohol can provide temporary mood alterations, excessive consumption can lead to mood swings and disrupt sleep. Consume these substances in moderation and be mindful of their effects on your mental well-being.

10. Nutrient Timing:

Consider the timing of your meals. Eating balanced meals and snacks throughout the day can help stabilize blood sugar levels and prevent mood fluctuations.

11. Seek Professional Guidance:

If you have specific dietary concerns or mental health conditions, consider consulting with a registered dietitian or mental health professional. They can provide personalized guidance tailored to your needs.

Sample Nutritional Strategies in Action:

◈ **Morning Fuel:** Start your day with a balanced breakfast that includes whole grains, lean protein, and fruits. This provides sustained energy and supports cognitive function.

◈ **Omega-3 Boost:** Enjoy a serving of fatty fish like salmon or a handful of walnuts a few times a week to boost your intake of omega-3 fatty acids.

◈ **Colorful Plates:** Incorporate a variety of colorful fruits and vegetables into your meals to maximize antioxidant intake.

◈ **Probiotic Snacks:** Include yogurt or kefir as a healthy snack option to support your gut microbiome.

◈ **Hydration Habit:** Carry a reusable water bottle with you to remind yourself to stay hydrated throughout the day.

◈ **Mindful Meals:** Practice mindful eating by setting aside time for meals, avoiding distractions, and savoring each bite.

Your Personal Nutritional Symphony

Your nutritional choices play a pivotal role in shaping your mental well-being. By composing a diet rich in essential nutrients and mindful eating practices, you can create a harmonious symphony of mental wellness. These nutritional strategies empower you to take charge of your emotional and cognitive health, one meal at a time.

The Impact of Hydration on Mood and Cognition

Imagine your body as a river, with clear, flowing water nourishing every aspect of your being. Hydration is the life force that keeps this river flowing smoothly. Here's how the impact of hydration on mood and cognition can be transformative:

1. Cognitive Function:

Water is essential for maintaining optimal cognitive function. Dehydration can impair your ability to concentrate, think clearly, and make decisions. Even mild dehydration can lead to cognitive deficits, including memory problems.

2. Mood Regulation:

Proper hydration is closely tied to mood regulation. Dehydration can lead to irritability, anxiety, and even feelings of sadness. When you're well-hydrated, you're better equipped to manage stress and maintain emotional balance.

3. Fatigue Reduction:

Dehydration can leave you feeling tired and lethargic. It's like a dimmer switch on your mental energy. Staying hydrated helps you feel more alert and focused, reducing the likelihood of mental fatigue.

4. Headache Prevention:

Headaches are a common symptom of dehydration. When you're well-hydrated, you're less likely to experience painful headaches, which can significantly impact your mood and overall well-being.

5. Stress Management:

Hydration supports your body's stress response. When you're adequately hydrated, your body can better regulate cortisol, the stress hormone. This helps you manage stress more effectively.

6. Electrolyte Balance:

Proper hydration helps maintain the balance of electrolytes in your body, including sodium and potassium. These electrolytes are essential for nerve function and muscle contractions, which are crucial for cognitive function and mood regulation.

7. Physical Activity and Hydration:

Physical activity, another critical aspect of mental well-being, increases your body's need for hydration. When you exercise, you lose fluids through sweat. Staying hydrated supports your physical activity goals, which, in turn, benefit your mental health.

8. Sleep Quality:

Hydration can impact sleep quality. Dehydration can lead to discomfort and nighttime awakenings. Adequate hydration supports better sleep, enhancing your mood and cognitive function during waking hours.

9. Mindful Hydration:

Practicing mindful hydration involves being aware of your body's signals for thirst and responding promptly. This mindfulness ensures that you stay adequately hydrated throughout the day.

10. Fluid Sources:

Remember that hydration isn't limited to water alone. Foods with high water content, such as fruits and vegetables, contribute to your daily fluid intake.

Sample Hydration Practices:

◈ **Set a Hydration Schedule:** Aim to drink water regularly throughout the day, even when you're not thirsty.

◈ **Monitor Urine Color:** Pay attention to the color of your urine. Pale yellow is a sign of good hydration, while dark yellow or amber may indicate dehydration.

◈ **Hydrate Before Physical Activity:** Drink water before, during, and after exercise to maintain fluid balance.

◈ **Limit Dehydrating Beverages:** Reduce consumption of beverages that can dehydrate you, such as caffeine and alcohol.

◈ **Hydrate Mindfully:** When you drink water, pause to savor each sip. Take a moment to appreciate the refreshing sensation.

Nourishing Your Mental River

Proper hydration is a foundational pillar of mental well-being. By recognizing the impact of hydration on mood and cognition and adopting mindful hydration practices, you can ensure that the river of vitality flows freely within you. Stay hydrated to support your cognitive function, emotional balance, and overall mental wellness.

Recipes and Meal Plans for a Balanced Mind

Imagine your kitchen as a laboratory for well-being, where you can craft meals that not only delight your taste buds but also elevate your mood and cognitive function. Here are some recipes and meal plans to help you achieve a balanced mind:

Morning Boost: Energizing Breakfast

Blueberry Almond Smoothie Bowl

Ingredients:

- ◈ 1 cup frozen blueberries

- ◈ 1/2 banana

- ◈ 1/4 cup Greek yogurt

- ◈ 1/4 cup almond milk

- ◈ 2 tablespoons almond butter

- ◈ 1 tablespoon honey (optional)

- ◈ Toppings: sliced almonds, fresh blueberries, chia seeds, and granola

Instructions:

1. Blend frozen blueberries, banana, Greek yogurt, almond milk, almond butter, and honey (if desired) until smooth.

2. Pour the smoothie into a bowl.

3. Top with sliced almonds, fresh blueberries, chia seeds, and granola.

4. Enjoy a nutrient-packed breakfast that provides antioxidants, healthy fats, and protein for sustained energy and mood support.

Lunchtime Delight: Brain-Boosting Salad

Spinach and Quinoa Salad with Lemon-Tahini Dressing

Ingredients:

- ◈ 2 cups baby spinach

◈ 1/2 cup cooked quinoa

◈ 1/4 cup chickpeas, drained and rinsed

◈ 1/4 cup diced cucumber

◈ 1/4 cup cherry tomatoes, halved

◈ 2 tablespoons crumbled feta cheese

◈ Lemon-Tahini Dressing: 2 tablespoons tahini, juice of 1 lemon, 1 clove minced garlic, 1 tablespoon olive oil, salt, and pepper to taste

Instructions:

1. In a bowl, combine baby spinach, cooked quinoa, chickpeas, cucumber, cherry tomatoes, and feta cheese.

2. In a separate small bowl, whisk together tahini, lemon juice, minced garlic, olive oil, salt, and pepper to create the dressing.

3. Drizzle the dressing over the salad and toss to coat.

4. This salad is packed with fiber, healthy fats, and nutrients to support mental clarity and focus.

Evening Serenity: Calming Dinner

Salmon with Roasted Vegetables and Quinoa

Ingredients:

◈ 2 salmon fillets

◈ 2 cups mixed vegetables (e.g., broccoli, bell peppers, carrots)

◈ 1 cup cooked quinoa

◈ 2 tablespoons olive oil

◈ 1 teaspoon dried herbs (e.g., rosemary, thyme)

◈ Salt and pepper to taste

◈ Lemon wedges for garnish

Instructions:

1. Preheat the oven to 375°F (190°C).

2. Place salmon fillets and mixed vegetables on a baking sheet.

3. Drizzle with olive oil and sprinkle with dried herbs, salt, and pepper.

4. Roast for 20-25 minutes or until salmon is cooked through and vegetables are tender.

5. Serve with cooked quinoa and garnish with lemon wedges.

6. This dinner provides omega-3 fatty acids, protein, and a variety of vegetables to support mood and brain health.

Weekly Meal Plan:

◈ **Day 1:**

◈ Breakfast: Blueberry Almond Smoothie Bowl

◈ Lunch: Spinach and Quinoa Salad with Lemon-Tahini Dressing

◈ Dinner: Salmon with Roasted Vegetables and Quinoa

◈ **Day 2:**

◈ Breakfast: Greek Yogurt Parfait with Berries and Almonds

◈ Lunch: Chickpea and Avocado Wrap

◈ Dinner: Vegetable Stir-Fry with Tofu and Brown Rice

◈ **Day 3:**

◈ Breakfast: Oatmeal with Banana and Walnuts

◈ Lunch: Lentil and Vegetable Soup

◈ Dinner: Grilled Chicken with Sweet Potato and Asparagus

◈ **Day 4:**

◈ Breakfast: Chia Seed Pudding with Mango and Coconut

◈ Lunch: Quinoa and Black Bean Bowl with Avocado

◈ Dinner: Baked Cod with Lemon and Herbs, served with Quinoa and Steamed Broccoli

Creating Balance, One Bite at a Time

These recipes and meal plans are designed to help you nourish your body and mind with wholesome ingredients. By incorporating these dishes into your daily life, you can create a harmonious balance that supports your mental well-being. Remember that a balanced diet is just one piece of the puzzle—physical activity, hydration, and mindfulness all play crucial roles in cultivating a holistic approach to mental wellness.

Chapter 11: The Social Aspect of Exercise

How Physical Activity Fosters Social Connections

Picture this: a group of people gathered on a sunny morning at the park, lacing up their running shoes and preparing for a jog together. Or a team of friends laughing and strategizing on the basketball court. These scenes exemplify how physical activity fosters social connections, providing a sense of belonging and support:

1. Shared Goals and Challenges:

Engaging in physical activity often means working towards a common goal or overcoming challenges together. Whether it's training for a marathon, conquering a hiking trail, or completing a fitness class, the shared experience bonds individuals and provides a sense of purpose.

2. Camaraderie and Support:

Physical activities create opportunities for camaraderie and mutual support. Team sports, group fitness classes, and workout buddies offer companionship, motivation, and encouragement. Sharing successes and setbacks can strengthen friendships and boost morale.

3. Community and Belonging:

Joining a sports league, club, or fitness group can introduce you to a community of like-minded individuals who share your interests. Being part of such a community fosters a sense of belonging and provides a social network.

4. Social Interaction and Fun:

Physical activities often involve social interaction and enjoyment. Whether it's chatting during a walk, dancing with friends, or playing a game, the fun and laughter that come with these activities enhance social bonds and contribute to positive emotional experiences.

5. Accountability and Consistency:

Having a workout buddy or group can provide accountability, making it more likely that you'll stick to your exercise routine. The commitment to others can be a powerful motivator for maintaining physical activity.

6. Diversity of Perspectives:

Engaging in physical activity with a variety of people exposes you to different perspectives and experiences. This diversity enriches your social interactions and broadens your horizons.

7. Reducing Social Isolation:

For individuals who may be at risk of social isolation, such as seniors or those dealing with mental health challenges, group-based physical activities offer a lifeline. They provide opportunities for regular social engagement and emotional support.

8. Building Trust and Cooperation:

Team sports, in particular, teach valuable life skills like trust, cooperation, and communication. These skills extend beyond the playing field and can positively impact relationships in other areas of life.

Sample Activities for Building Social Connections:

◈ Join a local sports league or recreational team.

◈ Attend group fitness classes at your gym or fitness center.

◈ Participate in charity walks, runs, or cycling events.

◈ Explore outdoor group activities like hiking or cycling clubs.

◈ Sign up for dance classes or group yoga sessions.

◈ Volunteer for community-based physical activity initiatives.

The Social Tapestry of Well-Being

Physical activity weaves the threads of social connections into the tapestry of well-being. By engaging in physical activities with others, you strengthen friendships, build communities, and experience the joy of shared accomplishments. These connections not only enhance your mental well-being but also provide a robust support system for life's challenges.

Group Fitness Classes and Their Mental Health Benefits

Imagine walking into a brightly lit studio filled with individuals of various ages and fitness levels, all gathered for a common purpose – to move, sweat, and improve their mental well-being. Here's how group fitness classes can become a sanctuary for your mind:

1. Motivation and Accountability:

Group fitness classes provide a structured environment with set schedules and instructors who guide you through the workout. This structure adds a level of accountability that can be challenging to maintain with solo exercise routines. Knowing that others are expecting you can be a powerful motivator.

2. Social Connection:

The group setting fosters social interaction. You'll meet people who share your fitness goals, and over time, these connections can evolve into friendships. The sense of belonging and camaraderie can boost your mood and reduce feelings of loneliness.

3. Diverse Workouts:

Fitness classes come in a wide variety of styles – from high-intensity interval training (HIIT) and spinning to yoga and dance. This diversity allows you to explore different forms of exercise and find what resonates with you. Trying new activities can add excitement to your fitness routine.

4. Expert Guidance:

Instructors are trained to lead classes effectively, ensuring that participants perform exercises correctly and safely. Their guidance can help you progress in your fitness journey and build confidence.

5. Stress Reduction:

Engaging in a fitness class can be a fantastic stress reliever. Physical activity triggers the release of endorphins, the body's natural mood lifters, which can help you unwind and reduce anxiety.

6. Routine and Structure:

Having a set class schedule can provide structure to your day or week, which is beneficial for mental well-being. Routine can create a sense of stability and predictability, reducing stress.

7. Positive Peer Pressure:

In a fitness class, you're surrounded by individuals who are all working toward their fitness goals. This positive peer pressure can encourage you to push your limits and achieve more than you might on your own.

8. Mind-Body Connection:

Many group fitness classes, such as yoga and Pilates, emphasize the mind-body connection. These practices can enhance mindfulness, improve focus, and help you manage emotions more effectively.

9. Achievement and Self-Esteem:

As you progress in your fitness journey and achieve personal milestones, your self-esteem and confidence receive a significant boost. Recognizing your physical capabilities can translate into increased self-belief in other areas of life.

10. Fun and Enjoyment:

Perhaps most importantly, group fitness classes are designed to be enjoyable. When exercise is fun, you're more likely to stick with it, leading to long-term mental health benefits.

Sample Group Fitness Class Options:

◈ **Spinning or Indoor Cycling:** A high-energy cardiovascular workout.

◈ **Zumba:** Dance-based fitness class that combines Latin and international music.

◈ **Yoga:** Focused on flexibility, strength, and relaxation.

◈ **Bootcamp:** A challenging full-body workout that often incorporates strength and cardio exercises.

◈ **Pilates:** Emphasizes core strength, flexibility, and posture.

◈ **HIIT:** High-intensity interval training for a quick, efficient workout.

A Community of Support

Group fitness classes offer a unique blend of physical activity, social connection, and motivation. They create a supportive community that can enhance your mental well-being by boosting your mood, reducing stress, and providing a sense of belonging. Whether you're a seasoned fitness enthusiast or new to exercise, these classes can become a vital part of your holistic approach to mental wellness.

Creating a Supportive Exercise Community

Imagine a place where you walk in, and a sense of encouragement and unity fills the air. This is the essence of a supportive exercise community. Here's how you can create and thrive within such a community:

1. Open and Inclusive Atmosphere:

Foster an atmosphere of inclusivity and openness. Encourage individuals of all fitness levels, backgrounds, and ages to join your exercise community. Make everyone feel welcome and valued.

2. Clear Goals and Values:

Define the goals and values of your exercise community. What do you aim to achieve together? Whether it's weight loss, strength building, or stress reduction, having a shared purpose unites the group.

3. Communication and Connection:

Effective communication is the glue that holds your community together. Create channels for members to interact, share their progress, and offer support. This can be a group chat, social media group, or regular meetings.

4. Group Activities:

Organize group activities and workouts. These can be fitness classes, outdoor hikes, charity runs, or simply meeting at the local park for a workout session. Group activities provide opportunities for bonding and shared experiences.

5. Positive Reinforcement:

Celebrate achievements, no matter how small. Offer positive reinforcement and recognition to members who reach their goals or show dedication to their fitness journey.

6. Accountability Partners:

Encourage members to pair up as accountability partners. Having someone to check in with can boost motivation and commitment.

7. Mentorship:

Establish mentorship programs within your community. Experienced members can mentor newcomers, offering guidance and support based on their own journey.

8. Diversity and Inclusion:

Embrace diversity within your exercise community. Different backgrounds and perspectives can enrich the group's experience and broaden everyone's horizons.

9. Empowerment and Education:

Promote a culture of empowerment and education. Share information on fitness, nutrition, and mental health. Knowledge empowers members to make informed choices.

10. Support Beyond Exercise:

Recognize that your exercise community is more than just a place to work out. It's a support system that extends beyond the gym or fitness class. Encourage members to be there for one another in times of need.

11. Regular Feedback:

Seek feedback from members on how to improve the community. Act on suggestions and continuously strive to make it a better, more supportive space.

Sample Activities for Building Community:

◇ **Theme Workouts:** Host themed workout sessions or challenges, such as holiday-themed workouts or fitness challenges for charity.

◇ **Social Events:** Organize non-exercise-related social events like picnics, potlucks, or movie nights to strengthen personal connections.

◇ **Guest Speakers:** Invite fitness experts, nutritionists, or mental health professionals to give talks or workshops.

◇ **Online Forums:** Create a private online forum or social media group for members to discuss their fitness journeys, share tips, and offer support.

The Power of Unity

A supportive exercise community is like a well-tended garden; it flourishes when nurtured with care and attention. Together, you can achieve fitness goals, enhance mental well-being, and create lasting friendships. The bonds you form within this community extend far beyond the physical benefits of exercise, enriching your life in numerous ways.

Personal Stories of Friendships Formed Through Fitness

Story 1: Sarah and Emily - Running Buddies for Life

Sarah and Emily never knew they would become best friends when they laced up their running shoes for the first time at a local charity run. Both were going through challenging times in their lives, dealing with personal setbacks and feeling isolated. Running brought them together, and the shared miles became a bridge to each other's hearts.

As they trained together, they talked about everything under the sun. They laughed, they cried, and they encouraged each other to keep going, both in their runs and in life. The finish line of that charity run marked the beginning of a deep and enduring friendship.

Through the years, Sarah and Emily have run countless races together, from 5Ks to marathons. They've also been each other's pillars of support during difficult moments. Their friendship, born on the road, has been a source of strength, laughter, and unwavering support. They know that no matter what life throws their way, they'll always have a running buddy for life.

Story 2: The Gym Gang - A Tight-Knit Fitness Family

In a bustling city, a group of individuals from diverse backgrounds found themselves in the same gym, chasing their fitness goals. They started as strangers but soon became inseparable. What began as casual greetings in between sets evolved into a tight-knit fitness family.

Together, they conquered the weights, the treadmills, and the challenges of life. They shared workout tips, swapped healthy recipes, and celebrated each other's achievements, big and small. The gym became their sanctuary, a place where they not only improved their physical health but also found unwavering support.

Through breakups, job changes, and personal triumphs, this gym gang has been there for one another. They've become more than just workout buddies; they're each other's confidants, cheerleaders, and, most importantly, friends who've transformed the gym into a place of camaraderie and inspiration.

Story 3: The Dance Crew - Healing Hearts Through Movement

In a local dance studio, a group of women of all ages and backgrounds came together to express themselves through dance. Each had her own story of struggles and triumphs, but they found solace and joy in the rhythm of movement.

As they learned new dance routines and choreography, they discovered the power of dance not only to transform their bodies but also to heal their hearts. The dance studio became a safe space where they could be themselves, let go of their worries, and dance away their stress.

Beyond the studio, they formed a sisterhood. They celebrated birthdays, attended each other's life events, and offered a shoulder to cry on when needed. The bond they created through dance transcended the studio walls, showing them that friendship can blossom in the most unexpected places.

Story 4: Mark and Jake - Lifelong Lifting Partners

Mark and Jake met in the weight room of their college gym. Both were aspiring bodybuilders, driven by a passion for fitness and a desire to push their physical limits. They began spotting each other, sharing workout routines, and challenging each other to lift heavier.

Their friendship deepened through their shared pursuit of strength and growth. They learned discipline, perseverance, and the importance of setting and achieving goals. Beyond the gym, they supported each other academically and emotionally, becoming not just lifting partners but true friends.

Years later, Mark and Jake still lift weights together. Their bond remains as strong as the muscles they've built. They know that their friendship, forged amidst the clanking of weights, is a testament to the transformative power of fitness and shared aspirations.

These stories highlight the incredible potential of fitness to bring people together, forming bonds that withstand the test of time and adversity. Friendships formed through fitness are not only about achieving physical goals; they're about the profound impact of human connection on mental well-being. These friendships serve as a reminder that the pursuit of a healthier body can lead to a happier heart and a richer life.

Chapter 12: Overcoming Plateaus and Challenges

Strategies for Breaking Through Fitness Plateaus

The Journey of Fitness: Peaks and Plateaus

Picture your fitness journey as a winding path, full of peaks and plateaus. While the peaks are exhilarating, the plateaus can be disheartening. But remember, plateaus are not the end of your journey; they are merely a pause. Here are some strategies to help you overcome them:

1. Change Your Routine:

One of the most common causes of plateaus is doing the same exercises and routines for an extended period. Your body adapts to this consistency, and progress stagnates. To break through, vary your workouts. Try different exercises, change the intensity, or explore new fitness classes.

2. Set New Goals:

Reignite your motivation by setting new, challenging goals. Having a clear target can provide the drive you need to push through a plateau. Whether it's running a faster mile, lifting heavier weights, or mastering a yoga pose, specific goals give your workouts purpose.

3. Periodization:

Periodization is a training technique that involves breaking your fitness routine into cycles with varying intensity levels. By strategically alternating between high-intensity and low-intensity periods, you can prevent plateaus and promote continuous improvement.

4. Nutrition Assessment:

Evaluate your nutrition habits. Sometimes, plateaus occur because your diet isn't supporting your fitness goals adequately. Consult with a nutritionist or dietitian to ensure you're fueling your body optimally.

5. Rest and Recovery:

Overtraining can lead to plateaus and even injury. Ensure you're getting enough rest and recovery time. Your body needs this downtime to repair and grow stronger.

6. Track Progress:

Keep a detailed record of your workouts, diet, and overall well-being. This allows you to identify patterns and make informed adjustments to your routine.

7. Seek Expert Guidance:

A personal trainer or fitness coach can provide invaluable guidance when you're stuck on a plateau. They can create a tailored workout plan, offer advice on nutrition, and monitor your progress.

8. Mindset Matters:

Remember that plateaus are a natural part of any fitness journey. Approach them with a positive mindset. Instead of seeing a plateau as a setback, view it as an opportunity to learn and grow.

9. Mix Up Your Cardio:

If you're primarily doing one type of cardio exercise, consider diversifying your cardiovascular activities. Swap out running for swimming, cycling, or dance. This not only challenges your body differently but keeps your workouts exciting.

10. Patience and Persistence:

Breaking through a plateau takes time and persistence. Don't get discouraged if progress is slower than you'd like. Keep your long-term goals in mind and stay committed to the process.

11. Celebrate Small Wins:

Even during a plateau, there are small victories to celebrate. Acknowledge and celebrate your achievements along the way. These moments of recognition can keep your motivation high.

Embracing Plateaus as Growth Opportunities

Remember that plateaus are part of the journey, not roadblocks that halt your progress indefinitely. They teach you patience, resilience, and the importance of adaptability. By implementing these strategies and maintaining a positive mindset, you can break through plateaus and continue your ascent toward your fitness goals.

Coping with Setbacks and Injuries

Setbacks and injuries are part of the terrain when you're on the path to better physical and mental health. They can be frustrating, disheartening, and even demotivating, but they are not the end of your journey. Here's how to cope and keep moving forward:

1. Acceptance and Mindfulness:

The first step in coping with setbacks and injuries is acceptance. Acknowledge that they are a part of life, and they can happen to anyone, regardless of their fitness level. Practicing mindfulness can help you stay present and calm during challenging times.

2. Seek Professional Help:

If you experience a significant injury, consult a healthcare professional, such as a physical therapist or sports medicine specialist. They can provide a proper diagnosis, treatment plan, and guidance for rehabilitation.

3. Modify Your Exercise Routine:

While recovering from an injury, it's crucial to modify your exercise routine to accommodate your limitations. Work closely with a physical therapist or trainer to develop a safe and effective plan that promotes healing without causing further harm.

4. Focus on Nutrition and Recovery:

During recovery, prioritize your nutrition and rest. Proper fuel and adequate sleep are essential for healing. Consider consulting a registered dietitian to ensure you're providing your body with the nutrients it needs to recover.

5. Mental Resilience:

Coping with setbacks requires mental resilience. Use the setback as an opportunity to build mental strength. Stay positive and remind yourself of your long-term goals.

6. Stay Connected:

Stay connected with your exercise community or workout buddies. They can provide emotional support and encouragement during your recovery period. Sometimes, just talking about your frustrations can be therapeutic.

7. Modify Goals:

While recovering, adjust your fitness goals to be more realistic and attainable given your current circumstances. Setting small, achievable milestones can provide a sense of accomplishment and motivation.

8. Explore Alternative Activities:

If your injury restricts your usual activities, explore alternative exercises that you can safely engage in. Aquatic therapy, chair yoga, or seated strength training are options that can maintain your fitness level while recovering.

9. Visualize and Stay Engaged:

Mental rehearsal through visualization can help maintain your connection to your fitness goals. Visualize your comeback and imagine yourself successfully achieving your goals once again.

10. Learn from the Experience:

Setbacks and injuries can teach valuable lessons about your body and fitness journey. Take the time to learn from your experience and make necessary adjustments to prevent similar issues in the future.

11. Celebrate Progress:

Even small steps forward are worth celebrating. Acknowledge and celebrate your progress as you recover. It's a testament to your resilience and determination.

12. Seek Professional Guidance for Mental Health:

If a setback or injury impacts your mental well-being, consider seeking the support of a mental health professional. They can provide strategies to manage stress, anxiety, or depression that may arise during your recovery.

The Comeback is Stronger Than the Setback

Setbacks and injuries are not signs of weakness; they are opportunities for growth, resilience, and learning. With the right mindset and support, you can overcome these challenges and emerge from them stronger and more determined than ever. Remember, the comeback is often more powerful than the setback.

Navigating Mental Hurdles in Your Fitness Journey

Your fitness journey is not just a physical endeavor; it's a mental one too. As you work toward your goals, you may encounter various mental hurdles. Here's how to navigate them with resilience and determination:

1. Self-Doubt and Negative Self-Talk:

Negative self-talk can be one of the most significant mental obstacles. When you catch yourself doubting your abilities or criticizing your progress, counter those thoughts with positive affirmations. Remind yourself of your past achievements and focus on your strengths.

2. Perfectionism:

Striving for perfection can lead to frustration and burnout. Understand that progress often involves setbacks and imperfections. Embrace the concept of progress, not perfection. Set realistic goals and celebrate your accomplishments along the way.

3. Fear of Failure:

The fear of failing or not meeting your own expectations can be paralyzing. Shift your mindset and view failure as an opportunity to learn and grow. Many successful individuals have experienced setbacks on their journeys to success.

4. Comparison and Envy:

Comparing yourself to others can diminish your self-esteem and motivation. Remember that everyone's journey is unique. Focus on your progress and celebrate your accomplishments, no matter how small they may seem.

5. Impatience:

It's natural to want results quickly, but impatience can lead to frustration. Understand that lasting change takes time. Break your long-term goals into smaller, manageable steps to maintain motivation.

6. Lack of Motivation:

There will be days when motivation wanes. On those days, focus on discipline and commitment rather than waiting for motivation to strike. Create a routine that becomes a habit, making it easier to stay on track.

7. Overthinking:

Overanalyzing your workouts, nutrition, or progress can lead to mental fatigue. Trust in your plan and the process. Overthinking can cloud your judgment and create unnecessary stress.

8. Stress and Anxiety:

Stress and anxiety can affect your ability to stay consistent with your fitness routine. Incorporate stress-reduction techniques such as meditation, deep breathing, or yoga into your routine to help manage these challenges.

9. Lack of Self-Compassion:

Be kind to yourself. Understand that setbacks and challenges are part of the journey. Treat yourself with the same kindness and compassion you would offer a friend facing similar difficulties.

10. Goal Alignment with Values:

Ensure that your fitness goals align with your values and personal aspirations. When your goals reflect what truly matters to you, it's easier to stay motivated and overcome mental hurdles.

11. Seek Support:

Don't hesitate to seek support from friends, family, or a mental health professional if you're struggling with persistent mental hurdles. Talking about your challenges can provide valuable insight and emotional relief.

12. Visualize Success:

Visualization can be a powerful tool. Take time to envision your success, whether it's achieving a specific fitness goal or experiencing improved mental well-being. Visualization can boost motivation and determination.

Remember, mental hurdles are a natural part of the journey to improved physical and mental health. By acknowledging them and implementing these strategies, you can strengthen your mental resilience and continue moving forward, even when faced with obstacles. Your mind is a powerful ally in your fitness journey, and with the right mindset, you can achieve your goals and enjoy lasting well-being.

Reinventing Your Routine for Long-Term Success

Your fitness journey is a dynamic and evolving adventure. To achieve long-term success, you must be willing to reinvent your routine. Here's how to keep your fitness journey exciting and aligned with your goals:

1. Goal Reflection:

Regularly revisit your fitness goals and assess whether they still resonate with your current priorities. Are your goals aligned with your values and aspirations? If not, consider adjusting them to reflect your evolving desires.

2. Variety is Key:

Inject variety into your workouts. Experiment with different exercises, classes, and activities. This not only prevents boredom but also challenges your body in new ways, promoting continuous improvement.

3. Change the Intensity:

Periodically modify the intensity of your workouts. Incorporate high-intensity intervals or low-intensity recovery periods to keep your body responsive to training stimuli.

4. Try New Activities:

Explore new physical activities that pique your interest. Whether it's dance, martial arts, rock climbing, or water aerobics, discovering new hobbies can rejuvenate your fitness journey.

5. Cross-Train:

Cross-training involves incorporating different types of exercises into your routine. This can help prevent overuse injuries and engage various muscle groups while keeping your workouts fresh.

6. Set Exciting Challenges:

Challenge yourself with exciting milestones or events, such as a fitness competition, charity run, or adventure race. Having a tangible goal on the horizon can reignite your motivation.

7. Learn New Skills:

Consider acquiring new fitness-related skills or certifications. Learning can be a motivating and fulfilling aspect of your fitness journey.

8. Seek Professional Guidance:

Consult with a personal trainer or fitness coach periodically. They can create a fresh and effective workout plan tailored to your evolving goals and fitness level.

9. Group Dynamics:

If you've been primarily exercising alone, try joining group classes or team sports. The camaraderie and shared experiences can be invigorating and foster a sense of community.

10. Embrace Technology:

Explore fitness apps, wearables, or online platforms that provide new workout routines, challenges, and tracking capabilities. Technology can add an exciting dimension to your fitness routine.

11. Mind-Body Connection:

Incorporate mind-body practices like yoga or tai chi into your routine. These practices not only enhance physical flexibility but also promote mental relaxation and mindfulness.

12. Listen to Your Body:

Pay close attention to your body's signals. If you're feeling fatigued or burned out, don't hesitate to take a break or adjust your routine to prioritize recovery.

13. Periodic Detox:

Consider a physical and mental "detox" period where you focus on simpler, less structured activities like walking, hiking, or simply enjoying nature. This can refresh your perspective on fitness.

14. Celebrate Milestones:

Celebrate your achievements and milestones along the way. Acknowledging your progress, no matter how small, reinforces your commitment to long-term success.

15. Reflect and Adapt:

Regularly reflect on your fitness journey. What worked? What didn't? What can you adjust for better results? Adaptation and continuous improvement are the keys to long-term success.

Remember, your fitness journey is a lifelong adventure filled with exciting opportunities for growth and self-discovery. Embrace change and evolution as essential elements of your path to lasting physical and mental well-being. With a willingness to reinvent your routine, you can enjoy a fulfilling and sustainable fitness journey.

Chapter 13: The Power of Rest and Recovery

The Importance of Rest in Mental Health

1. Stress Reduction:

Rest acts as a natural stress reducer. During sleep and relaxation, your body has the opportunity to lower stress hormones like cortisol. A well-rested mind is better equipped to handle daily stressors and challenges.

2. Emotional Regulation:

Sleep plays a crucial role in emotional regulation. Adequate rest helps stabilize mood and enhance emotional resilience. Without enough sleep, you may find yourself more irritable, anxious, or prone to mood swings.

3. Cognitive Function:

Rest is essential for optimal cognitive function. Sleep, in particular, is when your brain consolidates memories, processes emotions, and repairs itself. A well-rested mind is sharper, more focused, and better equipped for decision-making and problem-solving.

4. Creativity and Innovation:

Rest stimulates creativity and innovation. When you give your mind time to rest, it can wander, make connections between seemingly unrelated ideas, and generate fresh insights. Many breakthroughs and "Aha!" moments occur during periods of relaxation.

5. Energy and Motivation:

Rest replenishes your physical and mental energy reserves. Adequate sleep and relaxation leave you feeling refreshed and motivated to tackle your fitness goals and daily challenges.

6. Resilience:

Rest enhances your mental resilience. When you're well-rested, you're better prepared to handle setbacks, overcome mental hurdles, and stay committed to your fitness journey.

7. Self-Care and Boundaries:

Prioritizing rest is an act of self-care. It signifies that you value your well-being and mental health. Establishing boundaries around rest ensures that you maintain a healthy work-life-fitness balance.

8. Prevention of Burnout:

Consistently pushing yourself without adequate rest can lead to burnout, both physically and mentally. Burnout can derail your fitness progress and negatively impact your mental health. Regular rest helps prevent this exhaustion.

9. Quality of Life:

Ultimately, the quality of your life is profoundly affected by the quality of your mental health. Rest is a cornerstone of good mental health and contributes to a higher quality of life overall.

10. Holistic Well-Being:

Your fitness journey should be about holistic well-being, encompassing both your physical and mental health. By recognizing the vital role of rest in mental health, you can achieve a more balanced and fulfilling life.

Balancing Act: Rest and Activity

In your quest for better mental and physical health, remember that rest and activity are two sides of the same coin. Just as you commit to your workouts and physical activities, commit to quality rest and recovery as well. Prioritize sleep, relaxation, and mindfulness practices to ensure your mental health thrives alongside your physical well-being.

Techniques for Effective Recovery

1. Prioritize Sleep:

Quality sleep is one of the most potent recovery tools at your disposal. Aim for 7-9 hours of uninterrupted sleep each night to allow your body and mind to rejuvenate fully.

2. Nutrition for Recovery:

Nutrition plays a pivotal role in recovery. After a workout, consume a balanced meal or snack that includes a combination of carbohydrates, protein, and healthy fats. This helps replenish glycogen stores, repair muscles, and aid in overall recovery.

3. Hydration:

Staying hydrated is vital for recovery. Water helps transport nutrients to cells and removes waste products. Ensure you're drinking enough water throughout the day, especially after a workout.

4. Active Recovery:

Incorporate active recovery into your routine. Light activities like walking, yoga, or swimming can promote blood flow, reduce muscle soreness, and enhance flexibility.

5. Foam Rolling and Stretching:

Foam rolling and stretching can alleviate muscle tension and soreness. Spend time stretching major muscle groups and using a foam roller to release knots and tightness.

6. Massage Therapy:

Regular massages can improve circulation, reduce muscle tension, and enhance overall relaxation. Consider incorporating massage into your recovery routine, whether through professional therapists or self-massage techniques.

7. Mindfulness and Relaxation:

Practice mindfulness and relaxation techniques such as meditation, deep breathing exercises, or progressive muscle relaxation. These practices can reduce stress, promote mental recovery, and enhance overall well-being.

8. Ice Baths and Contrast Therapy:

Cold therapy, such as ice baths or contrast baths (alternating between hot and cold water), can reduce inflammation and accelerate recovery for sore muscles.

9. Compression Garments:

Compression garments like sleeves or socks can aid in muscle recovery by improving circulation and reducing swelling. They are particularly useful for post-workout recovery.

10. Rest Days:

Incorporate rest days into your weekly schedule. These are days when you intentionally avoid intense workouts to allow your body and mind to recover fully.

11. Listen to Your Body:

Pay attention to how your body feels. If you're feeling fatigued or notice signs of overtraining, adjust your routine or take additional rest as needed.

12. Plan Deload Weeks:

Every few weeks, plan a deload week where you reduce the intensity and volume of your workouts. Deload weeks give your body a break while maintaining consistency.

13. Stay Consistent:

Consistency in your recovery efforts is crucial. Incorporate recovery strategies into your routine as diligently as you do your workouts.

14. Time Management:

Allocate time for recovery just as you do for workouts. Recognize that recovery is a proactive investment in your overall well-being.

15. Professional Guidance:

Consider seeking guidance from a sports therapist, physiotherapist, or recovery specialist who can provide personalized recommendations based on your fitness goals and specific needs.

Remember that effective recovery is not a luxury but a necessity for your fitness journey. By incorporating these techniques into your routine, you can optimize your recovery and ensure that both your body and mind are in peak condition for your fitness goals. A holistic approach to recovery enhances your overall well-being, allowing you to enjoy lasting health benefits.

Sleep and Its Impact on Mood and Cognition

1. Mood Regulation:

Sleep plays a vital role in regulating your mood. A good night's sleep helps you manage stress more effectively and reduces irritability and mood swings. Conversely, inadequate sleep can lead to heightened emotional reactivity.

2. Emotional Resilience:

Quality sleep enhances your emotional resilience, allowing you to better cope with challenging situations. When you're well-rested, you're less likely to feel overwhelmed by stressors and more capable of maintaining a positive outlook.

3. Cognitive Performance:

Sleep is essential for cognitive performance. It enhances your ability to focus, concentrate, and make decisions. A well-rested mind is more alert and capable of handling complex mental tasks.

4. Memory Consolidation:

During sleep, your brain consolidates memories and processes information acquired during the day. This process is crucial for learning and retaining new information. Lack of sleep can impair your memory and learning abilities.

5. Problem Solving:

Adequate sleep enhances problem-solving skills and creativity. It allows your brain to make connections between seemingly unrelated concepts, leading to innovative thinking and more effective solutions to challenges.

6. Emotional Regulation:

Sleep influences your emotional regulation by balancing neurotransmitters in your brain. It helps maintain healthy levels of serotonin and dopamine, both of which are crucial for mood stability.

7. Hormone Balance:

Sleep affects hormone regulation, particularly those related to stress and appetite. Inadequate sleep can lead to increased cortisol levels (the stress hormone) and disruptions in hunger-regulating hormones like leptin and ghrelin.

8. Resilience to Negative Emotions:

A good night's sleep helps you maintain perspective when dealing with negative emotions. It can prevent the amplification of emotional responses to minor setbacks.

9. Preventing Mental Health Issues:

Consistent, quality sleep is a protective factor against the development of mental health issues such as depression and anxiety. It supports overall psychological well-being.

10. Physical Health Impact:

Sleep is interconnected with physical health. Poor sleep can lead to physical health issues like obesity, diabetes, and cardiovascular problems, which, in turn, can affect mood and cognition.

11. Stress Management:

Quality sleep enhances your ability to manage stress. It allows your brain to process and adapt to stressful situations more effectively.

12. Hormonal Balance:

Sleep is crucial for hormonal balance, including the production of growth hormone, which aids in tissue repair, muscle growth, and overall physical recovery.

13. Recovery and Repair:

During deep sleep, your body undergoes physical repair and maintenance processes. This includes muscle recovery and cell regeneration, which can impact your overall physical and mental well-being.

14. Prevention of Cognitive Decline:

Sufficient sleep may play a role in preventing age-related cognitive decline and neurodegenerative diseases such as Alzheimer's.

15. Overall Well-Being:

In summary, sleep is a cornerstone of mental well-being. It supports mood regulation, cognitive function, and overall mental health. Prioritizing quality sleep is one of the most powerful steps you can take in your fitness journey and your quest for lasting well-being.

Personal Accounts of Transformation Through Rest

Meet Sarah: From Burnout to Bliss

Sarah's story is a testament to the transformative power of rest. As a dedicated professional with a thriving career and a passion for fitness, she had always pushed herself to excel in all aspects of her life. She was a regular at the gym, juggling work, family, and her personal goals with unwavering determination.

However, as the years went by, Sarah noticed a gradual decline in her mood and cognitive abilities. She was frequently irritable, struggled to concentrate at work, and experienced emotional fluctuations that took a toll on her relationships. Despite her commitment to her fitness routine, something was amiss.

It wasn't until a trusted friend gently pointed out the signs of burnout that Sarah began to reconsider her approach to her fitness journey and overall well-being. She decided to prioritize rest as a fundamental aspect of her routine.

Sarah started with small changes. She began to carve out time for relaxation and adopted mindfulness practices before bedtime. She created a sleep-friendly environment in her bedroom, minimizing distractions and establishing a consistent sleep schedule. Sarah also integrated restorative activities like meditation and gentle yoga into her fitness regimen.

Over time, Sarah's commitment to rest yielded remarkable results. Her mood stabilized, and she found herself more emotionally resilient in the face of stressors. Her cognitive abilities sharpened, enabling her to excel at work and pursue new challenges with enthusiasm. She even noticed improvements in her fitness performance, as her body responded positively to the added focus on rest and recovery.

But the most significant transformation was in Sarah's overall well-being. She felt more content, balanced, and fulfilled in her life. Her personal relationships flourished, and she approached her fitness journey with a newfound sense of joy and purpose. Sarah's story serves as a reminder that rest is not a sign of weakness but a powerful catalyst for transformation and lasting well-being.

Jake's Journey: Overcoming Mental Hurdles Through Rest

Jake's fitness journey had always been a source of pride and accomplishment. He was passionate about strength training and pushing his limits in the gym.

However, as time passed, he found himself grappling with mental hurdles that threatened to derail his progress.

Jake experienced periods of extreme fatigue, irritability, and emotional exhaustion. He couldn't understand why his once-beloved workouts were becoming a source of stress rather than joy. His goals seemed increasingly out of reach, and he felt trapped in a cycle of self-doubt and frustration.

It wasn't until Jake sought guidance from a fitness coach that he realized the importance of rest and recovery in his journey. His coach emphasized that rest wasn't a sign of weakness but a necessary component of progress and mental well-being.

Jake began to prioritize rest as part of his routine. He introduced structured rest days and incorporated active recovery activities like walking and stretching. He also focused on sleep hygiene, creating a sleep-friendly environment and committing to a consistent sleep schedule.

As he embraced the power of rest and recovery, Jake experienced a remarkable transformation. His mood stabilized, and he found renewed motivation for his fitness goals. The mental hurdles that had once plagued him began to dissipate, and he felt a sense of mental clarity and focus he hadn't experienced in years.

Today, Jake views rest as an essential part of his fitness journey. It has not only improved his physical performance but also his mental well-being. His story serves as a reminder that rest is a valuable tool for overcoming mental hurdles and achieving lasting fitness success.

These personal accounts underscore the transformative impact of rest on mental well-being. Prioritizing rest is not a sign of weakness but a vital strategy for optimizing your fitness journey and enjoying a higher quality of life.

Chapter 14: Monitoring Progress and Celebrating Success

The Role of Tracking Tools and Apps

1. Goal Clarity:

Tracking tools and apps help you define clear, specific fitness and mental health goals. Whether it's weight loss, muscle gain, improved sleep, or reduced stress, these tools allow you to set measurable objectives.

2. Accountability:

Using tracking tools creates a sense of accountability. When you record your progress, you're more likely to stick to your exercise routine and make healthier choices in your daily life.

3. Data-Driven Decisions:

Data is powerful. Tracking tools provide data on your workouts, nutrition, sleep patterns, and more. This information empowers you to make informed decisions about your fitness and mental well-being.

4. Motivation and Consistency:

Seeing your progress over time can be incredibly motivating. Tracking apps allow you to visualize your accomplishments, reinforcing your commitment to your fitness journey.

5. Identifying Patterns:

Tracking tools help you identify patterns in your behavior and habits. For example, you might notice that your mood improves on days when you exercise or that your sleep quality declines after late-night screen time. This awareness can lead to positive changes.

6. Personalized Plans:

Many tracking apps offer personalized workout and nutrition plans based on your goals and progress. These plans ensure that your fitness routine aligns with your mental health objectives.

7. Goal Adjustments:

As you track your progress, you can adjust your goals based on what's working and what isn't. This adaptability is essential for long-term success.

8. Social Support:

Some tracking apps allow you to connect with a community of like-minded individuals. Sharing your progress and challenges with others can provide a strong support system.

9. Celebrating Milestones:

Tracking tools make it easy to celebrate milestones along your journey. Whether it's a new personal best in the gym or consistently meeting your daily step count, recognizing your achievements boosts motivation.

10. Mindfulness and Self-Awareness:

Recording your physical activity, nutrition, and mental well-being encourages mindfulness. It prompts you to reflect on your choices and their impact on your overall health.

11. Stress Reduction:

Managing your fitness and mental health with tracking tools can reduce stress. Knowing that you're taking proactive steps toward your goals can alleviate anxiety.

12. Goal Visualization:

Tracking allows you to visualize your goals. You can set reminders and create vision boards within apps, helping you maintain focus on your objectives.

13. Adaptability:

Your fitness and mental health journey is not static. Tracking tools enable you to adapt to changes in your goals, lifestyle, and circumstances.

14. Comprehensive Insights:

Many tracking apps provide comprehensive insights into your well-being, including sleep quality, heart rate variability, and stress levels. These insights contribute to a holistic understanding of your health.

15. Long-Term Sustainability:

Ultimately, tracking tools contribute to the long-term sustainability of your fitness journey. They help you make gradual, sustainable changes that benefit your mental and physical well-being.

Incorporating tracking tools and apps into your fitness and mental health routine can be a game-changer. They provide the structure and data-driven insights needed to make informed decisions, stay motivated, and celebrate your progress along the way. As you continue your journey, remember that it's not just about reaching your destination but enjoying the entire path and celebrating each step forward.

Setting Achievable Milestones

1. Direction and Focus:

Milestones provide a clear sense of direction. When you set achievable milestones, you know where you're headed and can focus your efforts accordingly.

2. Motivation Boost:

Achieving a milestone, no matter how small, is incredibly motivating. It offers a sense of accomplishment that fuels your determination to continue.

3. Measuring Progress:

Milestones serve as markers for measuring your progress. They help you track how far you've come and how much closer you are to your ultimate goals.

4. Tangible Goals:

Achievable milestones make your goals tangible. Instead of aiming for something abstract like "better mental health," you can aim for specific accomplishments, such as reducing stress through daily mindfulness practice.

5. Celebrating Success:

Each milestone reached is an opportunity to celebrate success. These celebrations boost your morale and reinforce the positive habits and choices you've made.

6. Encouraging Consistency:

Having milestones in place encourages consistency. Regular effort and commitment are necessary to reach your milestones, fostering healthy habits along the way.

7. Adaptability:

Milestones can be adjusted as needed. If you find that a particular goal isn't realistic, you can modify it to better suit your circumstances or priorities.

8. Building Confidence:

Achieving milestones builds confidence in your abilities. As you accomplish each one, you gain confidence in your capacity to overcome challenges and achieve your long-term goals.

9. Preventing Overwhelm:

Breaking down your larger fitness and mental health goals into achievable milestones prevents overwhelm. It allows you to tackle one step at a time instead of feeling daunted by the bigger picture.

10. Enhancing Self-Reflection:

Milestones prompt self-reflection. They encourage you to assess what's working and what's not, helping you make necessary adjustments to your approach.

11. Building Resilience:

Working toward milestones can build resilience. It teaches you to persevere through setbacks and challenges, knowing that they are part of the journey.

12. Balancing Short-Term and Long-Term Goals:

Milestones help you strike a balance between short-term and long-term goals. While you focus on achieving smaller milestones, you're also progressing toward your ultimate objectives.

13. Personalized Goals:

Setting achievable milestones allows you to tailor your fitness and mental health goals to your unique circumstances and aspirations.

14. Maintaining Commitment:

Knowing that you have milestones to reach helps maintain your commitment to your fitness journey. It reminds you why you started and why your goals are important.

15. Enjoying the Journey:

Ultimately, milestones make the journey itself more enjoyable. They provide a sense of purpose and satisfaction along the way, making the process as fulfilling as the destination.

When setting achievable milestones, consider factors such as specificity, measurability, and relevance to your overall goals. Milestones should be challenging yet attainable, keeping you engaged and motivated as you progress. As you continue on your fitness and mental health journey, remember that each milestone reached is a testament to your determination and a step closer to the healthier, happier you that you're striving to become.

Celebrating Small Victories Along the Way

1. Motivation Reinforcement:

Each small victory serves as a reminder of your progress and a boost of motivation to continue. Celebrating these moments rekindles your enthusiasm for your fitness and mental health goals.

2. Positive Reinforcement:

Celebrating small victories reinforces the positive behaviors and choices that led to those achievements. It encourages you to maintain those habits and make them a permanent part of your lifestyle.

3. Improved Mood:

Acknowledging your successes releases dopamine, the brain's "feel-good" chemical. This can enhance your mood and overall sense of well-being.

4. Building Confidence:

Small victories build confidence in your ability to achieve larger goals. They prove that you have the skills and determination necessary for success.

5. Stress Reduction:

Positive celebrations can reduce stress and anxiety. They provide a welcome break from the pressures of striving for long-term goals.

6. Sustained Effort:

Recognizing your progress keeps your commitment strong. It reminds you that your efforts are paying off, even if the ultimate goal is still a work in progress.

7. Cultivating Gratitude:

Celebrating small victories encourages gratitude. It prompts you to appreciate the positive changes in your life and focus on what's going well.

8. Long-Term Perspective:

Small victories help you maintain a long-term perspective. They remind you that your fitness journey is not just about the destination but about the journey itself.

9. Emotional Resilience:

Acknowledging small victories fosters emotional resilience. It helps you bounce back from setbacks and challenges with a positive mindset.

10. Incremental Progress:

Success is often achieved through incremental progress. Small victories are the building blocks of larger achievements, so it's essential to celebrate them.

11. Self-Reflection:

Celebrations offer moments of self-reflection. They prompt you to assess what's working well and what you can improve as you move forward.

12. Personal Growth:

Your fitness journey isn't just about physical health; it's about personal growth. Celebrating small victories acknowledges the growth and development you've achieved.

13. Connection with Goals:

Each small victory is a connection to your overarching goals. Celebrating these moments reinforces your commitment to your fitness and mental health objectives.

14. Inspiration for Others:

Your journey can inspire others. When you celebrate small victories, you may motivate friends and family to embark on their own wellness journeys.

15. Enjoying the Process:

Ultimately, celebrating small victories makes the journey more enjoyable. It transforms your fitness path into a series of fulfilling and motivating moments.

Whether it's reaching a new personal best in the gym, consistently practicing mindfulness for a week, or making healthier food choices for a month, each small victory deserves recognition. It's these moments that will keep you moving forward, step by step, on your path to lasting health and well-being. Remember that success is not just about reaching the summit; it's about savoring every step of the climb.

Maintaining a Positive Outlook on Your Journey

Maintaining a positive outlook on your fitness and mental health journey is a cornerstone of lasting success. Here's why your mindset matters:

1. Resilience: A positive outlook equips you with the resilience to overcome setbacks and challenges. You view these obstacles as opportunities for growth rather than insurmountable barriers.

2. Motivation: Positivity fuels your motivation. When you maintain a positive mindset, you're more eager to take on challenges, push your limits, and stay committed to your goals.

3. Problem-Solving: A positive mindset enhances your problem-solving abilities. You approach challenges with a solution-oriented attitude, finding creative ways to overcome them.

4. Emotional Well-Being: Positivity is closely linked to emotional well-being. It reduces stress, anxiety, and depression, creating a foundation for mental health.

5. Self-Belief: A positive outlook strengthens your self-belief. You have faith in your ability to make positive changes in your life, which can be a self-fulfilling prophecy.

6. Increased Energy: Positivity generates energy. You approach your fitness routines and daily activities with enthusiasm, leading to improved physical and mental vitality.

7. Adaptability: Positivity fosters adaptability. You're more open to trying new approaches, experimenting with different strategies, and adjusting your goals as needed.

8. Healthy Relationships: A positive mindset enhances your relationships. You're more pleasant to be around, and your optimism can be contagious, spreading positivity to those around you.

9. Focus on Solutions: A positive outlook shifts your focus from problems to solutions. Instead of dwelling on the negatives, you concentrate on what you can do to improve your situation.

10. Persistence: Positivity encourages persistence. You're more likely to keep working toward your goals, even when progress is slow or challenging.

11. Enjoyment: A positive mindset makes the journey enjoyable. You find satisfaction in the process, not just the end result.

12. Goal Achievement: Positivity is linked to achieving your goals. When you believe in your ability to succeed, you're more likely to take the actions necessary to reach those goals.

13. Self-Care: Maintaining a positive outlook encourages self-care. You prioritize your physical and mental well-being because you value yourself and your journey.

14. Gratitude: Positivity often goes hand in hand with gratitude. You appreciate the progress you've made and the opportunities that come your way.

15. Mindfulness: A positive mindset aligns with mindfulness. You're present in the moment, savoring each step of your journey rather than anxiously rushing toward your destination.

Cultivating and sustaining a positive outlook requires practice and self-awareness. It involves consciously choosing to focus on the good, acknowledge your achievements, and approach challenges with a constructive attitude.

Chapter 15: Beyond the Finish Line: Maintaining Mental Wellness

Transitioning from a Fitness Journey to a Lifestyle

Transitioning from a fitness journey to a mental wellness lifestyle involves a deep and holistic approach. Here's a comprehensive look at how to make this pivotal shift:

1. Integration of Habits:

As you wrap up your fitness journey, focus on integrating the habits you've cultivated into your daily life. Whether it's regular exercise, mindfulness practices, or healthy eating, these habits should become second nature.

2. Long-Term Goals:

Shift your mindset from short-term goals to long-term mental wellness. Rather than aiming for a specific weight or fitness level, prioritize maintaining a balanced, resilient, and positive state of mind.

3. Mindful Eating:

Continue to make mindful choices in your nutrition. Emphasize a diet rich in whole foods, lean proteins, fruits, and vegetables, supporting both physical and mental health.

4. Sustainable Exercise:

Opt for exercise routines that you genuinely enjoy and can sustain over the long haul. Consistency is key, so choose activities that bring you joy and fit seamlessly into your lifestyle.

5. Holistic Well-Being:

Recognize that mental wellness goes beyond physical fitness. It encompasses emotional, social, and spiritual well-being. Dedicate time to nurturing these aspects of your life.

6. Stress Management:

Continue to prioritize stress management techniques, such as meditation, deep breathing, and progressive muscle relaxation. Regularly practice these skills to build emotional resilience.

7. Support Network:

Maintain connections with the support network you've built during your fitness journey. Friends, family, or fitness partners can provide encouragement and motivation.

8. Self-Care Rituals:

Incorporate self-care rituals into your routine. These can include journaling, spa days, nature walks, or any activities that promote relaxation and self-reflection.

9. Continuing Education:

Stay informed and open to learning about mental wellness. Attend workshops, read books, and seek out resources that help you deepen your understanding and practice.

10. Set New Goals:

Though you've reached milestones in your fitness journey, it's essential to set new mental wellness goals. These could involve cultivating more profound mindfulness, improving emotional intelligence, or nurturing healthier relationships.

11. Regular Assessment:

Periodically assess your mental well-being. Reflect on your emotions, stress levels, and overall contentment. If you notice any signs of imbalance, take proactive steps to address them.

12. Flexibility and Adaptation:

Recognize that life is full of changes and challenges. Your mental wellness routine should be adaptable. Be prepared to adjust your strategies as needed.

13. Gratitude Practice:

Incorporate a gratitude practice into your daily life. Take a moment each day to reflect on the positive aspects of your journey and your life as a whole.

14. Community Involvement:

Consider becoming involved in mental wellness communities or support groups. Sharing your experiences and insights can be beneficial for both you and others.

15. Celebration of Progress:

Finally, celebrate your ongoing progress. Each day that you prioritize your mental wellness is a victory. Acknowledge and honor your dedication to a healthier, happier, and more fulfilled life.

The transition from a fitness journey to a mental wellness lifestyle is a remarkable and transformative phase. It signifies the shift from a singular focus on physical health to a holistic approach that encompasses your mental and emotional well-being. Embrace this transition with enthusiasm, and know that by doing so, you're laying the foundation for a life of enduring mental wellness and vibrant overall health.

Strategies for Maintaining Mental Health Gains

Maintaining mental health gains involves a commitment to continued growth and well-being. Here are key strategies to ensure that your mental wellness remains a priority in your life:

1. Consistency is Key:

Consistency in your mental wellness practices is paramount. Just as you maintained a regular fitness routine, continue to prioritize mindfulness, stress management, and self-care on a consistent basis.

2. Mindful Reflection:

Regularly engage in mindful reflection on your mental well-being. Take time to assess your emotional state, stress levels, and overall contentment. Use this self-awareness to make any necessary adjustments.

3. Set and Revise Goals:

Set new mental wellness goals that align with your evolving needs and aspirations. These goals can focus on areas like emotional resilience, self-compassion, or deeper mindfulness practices.

4. Self-Compassion:

Practice self-compassion in your daily life. Treat yourself with the same kindness and understanding that you would offer to a friend facing challenges.

5. Seek Professional Guidance:

If needed, don't hesitate to seek professional guidance. Mental health professionals can provide valuable insights and strategies to help you maintain your gains.

6. Support Network:

Stay connected with your support network. Friends, family, and like-minded individuals can provide encouragement and accountability as you continue your mental wellness journey.

7. Adaptability:

Be flexible and adaptable in your approach to mental wellness. Life is dynamic, and your strategies may need adjustment based on changing circumstances.

8. Positive Affirmations:

Incorporate positive affirmations into your daily routine. These affirmations can help reinforce your commitment to mental wellness and boost your self-esteem.

9. Maintain Physical Health:

Remember that physical health and mental well-being are interconnected. Continue to prioritize exercise, nutrition, and sleep as they significantly impact your mood and cognitive function.

10. Self-Care Rituals:

Maintain and expand your self-care rituals. These activities can be a source of comfort and rejuvenation, promoting emotional well-being.

11. Gratitude Practice:

Continue your gratitude practice. Regularly reflect on the positive aspects of your life and your journey towards better mental health.

12. Stress Management:

Practice stress management techniques consistently. Whether it's meditation, deep breathing, or progressive muscle relaxation, these tools remain essential.

13. Education and Growth:

Keep educating yourself on mental wellness. Attend workshops, read books, and stay informed about the latest developments in the field.

14. Celebrate Milestones:

Celebrate your ongoing milestones in mental wellness. Each day you prioritize your well-being is a victory and an opportunity for celebration.

15. Enjoy the Journey:

Lastly, remember that mental wellness is not just about the destination; it's about enjoying the journey. Embrace the process, savor each moment, and cultivate a life filled with meaning, joy, and lasting mental well-being.

These strategies, when integrated into your daily life, will ensure that the mental health gains you've achieved through your fitness journey are not fleeting but instead become a permanent and enriching part of your lifelong well-being. Continue to invest in yourself, your mental wellness, and your overall health as you embark on this transformative transition.

Encouraging Others to Embark on Their Journey

Encouraging others to embark on their journey towards mental wellness is a gift you can give that extends the benefits of your own transformation. Here's how you can inspire and support others on their path:

1. Share Your Story:

Begin by sharing your personal journey towards mental wellness. Talk openly about the challenges you faced, the strategies that worked for you, and the positive impact it had on your life.

2. Be a Role Model:

Lead by example. Demonstrate your commitment to mental wellness through your daily habits and choices. Your consistency and positivity can inspire others to follow suit.

3. Offer Empathy and Understanding:

Be a compassionate listener when others express their struggles or concerns about their mental health. Your empathetic presence can provide comfort and encouragement.

4. Provide Resources:

Share resources and information on mental wellness. Recommend books, apps, workshops, or professionals that have been instrumental in your journey.

5. Encourage Small Steps:

Emphasize that progress doesn't have to be immediate or dramatic. Encourage others to take small, manageable steps towards their mental well-being.

6. Create a Supportive Environment:

Foster a supportive and non-judgmental environment where people feel safe discussing their mental health. Encourage open conversations about well-being.

7. Be Patient:

Recognize that everyone's journey is unique, and progress may take time. Be patient and offer ongoing support without pressure.

8. Celebrate Their Wins:

Acknowledge and celebrate the milestones and victories in others' mental wellness journeys, no matter how small they may seem.

9. Offer Encouragement:

Provide words of encouragement and motivation. Let others know that you believe in their ability to overcome challenges and thrive.

10. Share Mindfulness Practices:

Introduce mindfulness practices and exercises that have benefited you. Encourage others to explore these techniques to enhance their mental well-being.

11. Normalize Self-Care:

Normalize self-care as an essential aspect of overall health. Encourage self-care rituals and practices that nurture the mind, body, and soul.

12. Be a Source of Inspiration:

Share inspiring stories of individuals who have transformed their mental well-being. These stories can serve as beacons of hope and motivation.

13. Offer a Listening Ear:

Be available to listen without judgment whenever someone needs to talk. Sometimes, just knowing that someone cares can make a significant difference.

14. Encourage Seeking Professional Help:

If someone's mental health journey requires professional guidance, encourage them to seek help without stigma or shame.

15. Lead with Positivity:

Radiate positivity in your interactions and communications. Your optimism can be infectious and uplifting.

Your willingness to encourage and support others on their mental wellness journeys can have a profound impact on their lives. By sharing your experiences and insights, you empower them to embark on a transformative path towards greater well-being. Remember that the journey towards mental wellness is not only about personal growth but also about the positive ripple effect it can create in the lives of those you touch with your encouragement and wisdom.

A Final Call to Action for the Reader

As we conclude this journey through the world of mental wellness and the profound impact of physical activity, I extend to you a final call to action—a powerful reminder of the potential for transformation that lies within your reach.

Dear Reader,

You've embarked on a remarkable journey, exploring the intricate connection between physical activity and mental well-being. Throughout these chapters, you've delved into the science, the stories, and the strategies that can empower you to live a life of lasting mental wellness.

Now, as we stand at the precipice of the final chapter, I invite you to reflect on your own journey. You've gained insights into the power of consistency, the significance of self-care, and the profound impact of a positive mindset. You've learned how small steps can lead to great strides and how celebrating victories, no matter how modest, can fuel your motivation.

But the beauty of this journey lies not only in the transformation you've witnessed within yourself but also in the potential to inspire transformation in others. The wisdom you've acquired is a beacon of hope that can light the way for those still seeking their path to mental wellness.

So, I urge you to embrace your role as a torchbearer of well-being. Share your story, your experiences, and your newfound knowledge with those around you.

Be the catalyst for change, the hand that reaches out to lift others up, and the voice that encourages them to take the first step on their journey.

It's time to pay it forward, to create a ripple effect of mental wellness that touches the lives of friends, family, and communities. Be the friend who listens without judgment, the mentor who provides guidance, and the advocate for mental health.

As you do, remember that this journey is not one with a final destination. It's a lifelong pursuit—a commitment to nurturing your mental wellness and inspiring others to do the same. It's about creating a world where mental health is valued and prioritized, where resilience and positivity are celebrated, and where each individual has the tools to build a life of fulfillment and well-being.

So, my dear reader, let this be your final call to action: Be the spark of change, the beacon of hope, and the unwavering advocate for mental wellness. Together, we can create a world where the power of physical activity for mental health is celebrated, where the stigma around mental health is erased, and where well-being is within everyone's reach.

Your journey towards mental wellness continues, and it's a journey that can lead to a brighter, more resilient, and more fulfilled life. Thank you for joining me on this path, and may your dedication to mental wellness be a source of inspiration for yourself and countless others.

With warmest regards,

Gabriella Goldberger

Don't miss out!

Visit the website below and you can sign up to receive emails whenever Gabriella Goldberger publishes a new book. There's no charge and no obligation.

https://books2read.com/r/B-A-CNJAB-LXLOC

BOOKS 2 READ

Connecting independent readers to independent writers.

Also by Gabriella Goldberger

Mindful Eating: Nourish Your Well-Being
Holistic Approaches to Stress Management
Nutrition and Immune Health
The Connection Between Sleep and Health
85 Remarkable Women in History
Mindful Motion: The Path to Lasting Mental Wellness

www.ingramcontent.com/pod-product-compliance
Lightning Source LLC
Chambersburg PA
CBHW071323150726
47997CB00002B/583